Rock Clin

Contents

About This Book

The way of learning the sport of rock climbing has changed considerably in past decades. While 20 years ago the first steps toward climbing were taken almost exclusively on natural rock surfaces—on crags, also called climbing gardens— nowadays the beginner uses mainly an indoor-climbing gym: available at all times and in any weather, always safe but still exciting. Eventually, however, almost every one of those indoor climbers feels the urge to combine climbing fun with nature. They want to swap the plastic grips for the varied structures of real rock and not be limited by the ceiling, but rather view the unending sky above them and experience the impressive feeling of looking down from on high. Because there are many climbing gardens and well-established climbing crags about, the first step out of the climbing gym and onto the rocks—apart from the journey to get there—is nowadays easy.

Lead climbing—a distinct variation between indoor climbing with a top rope and Alpine rock climbing—promises more intense climbing while also challenging your ability and your psyche.

This book is devoted exclusively to the basics of rock climbing. So that lead climbing is made as safe as possible, the first section of the book covers the necessary basic knowledge required for climbing (e.g., protection and belay techniques, creating belay stands, and rappelling). We also cover climbing of multiple rope lengths (also called multi-pitch) and important subjects such as falling and bailing out from climbs. On purpose, we do not cover Alpine climbing and solo climbing. These subjects are too complicated for the beginner lead climber and would be too lengthy for a compact reference book.

Regardless of your reasons for taking up rock climbing, this book gives useful, valuable tips not only for climbing up but also for a safe descent. The experienced top-rope climber who has left the climbing gym behind and wants to take the first steps on the "sharp end" of the rope will also find comprehensive instructions. The "weekend-hobby climbers" (i.e., those who do not climb regularly) can use this book to review various tactics and bring their own knowledge up to speed.

This book does not intend to replace an established climbing school. We strongly recommend that your first step is to attend a course on lead climbing. In Europe, these are run by various Alpine clubs and mountain schools; there are similar organizations elsewhere in the world. In our opinion, a lead-climbing course in the climbing gym is not sufficient to prepare you for your first outdoor climbing experience. The knowledge required for outdoor rocks is more complex than what the limited possibilities available in the gym can offer.

"The brain is the most important muscle for climbing" (Güllich, cited in Hepp, 2004). This statement by Wolfgang Güllich (1960-1992)—a famous German climber and one of the first who brought extreme solo climbing to the Alps—is as valid today as ever.

With this in mind, we wish you many successful, safe, relaxing, but nevertheless exciting rock climbing experiences.

Just as rock climbing is not possible without a reliable partner, this book would not have been possible without the commitment and help of family and friends. We extend our hearty thanks to them and in particular Andrea, Christiane, Lukas and Peppi. Also we greatly thank Norbert and Bengt Haunerland for their help with the translation of the German original into English.

Detlef Heise-Flecken and Gabi Flecken

1 Equipment and Safety Techniques

1.1 Equipment Indoor Climbing

For indoor climbing, you need to have the following equipment:

- Climbing harness
- Climbing shoes
- Belay device with a HMS carabiner
- Climbing rope
- Chalk bag

Beginners should not buy a complete set of equipment immediately. In most cases, when first attempting climbing under the guidance and support of an instructor, you can rent the necessary climbing equipment from the climbing gym. Often, this is included in the initial fee for a beginners course. With a little experience, novice climbers can better assess what equipment is appropriate and necessary for them. Advice from instructors and advanced climbers can also be useful, although their advice sometimes tends toward personal favorites or trendy brands that are often very expensive and not necessarily the best choice for beginners. Because of the large number of products available, climbing equipment is now much more affordable. Extra care is required when purchasing used equipment, especially for inexperienced climbers who may not be able to evaluate wear and tear of such equipment.

This is particularly important with equipment that is offered through the internet, since neither the condition or size and fit can be checked prior to purchase. All safety-relevant equipment is subject to special standards indicated by the standardization marks EN, CE, and UIAA, and one of these must be marked on the article. It cannot be overemphasized that all climbing equipment must be handled carefully – your life and safety depend on it.

Rock Climbing

Climbing Harness

Sport climbers, nowadays, generally use a seat harness (photo 1). Full-body harnesses are only used by Alpine climbing groups carrying large backpacks as well as children under 8 because of their body size (see photo 2); sometimes these harnesses are also used for obstacle climbing (like crate climbing). Seat harnesses come in many different designs and prices. Always ensure your harness fits correctly and comfortably.

1

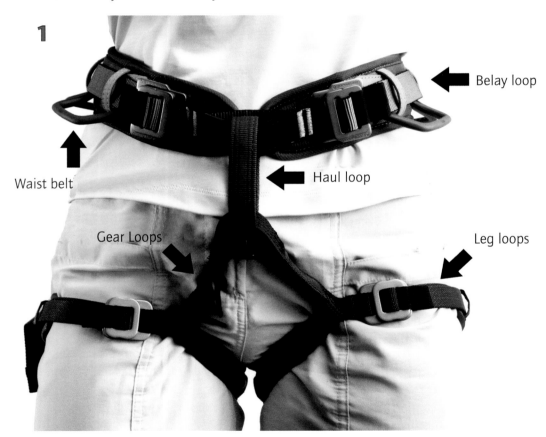

Belay loop

Waist belt

Haul loop

Gear Loops

Leg loops

Adjustable leg straps, while not necessary, are practical if, for example, you plan to wear thick pants as well as shorts, or you gain or loose weight over time. If harnesses are obtained for use in schools or other educational establishments, variability, ease of handling, and similarity are key. Meanwhile, fast adjust buckle systems (photo 3) that make the often tedious looping back of the buckle strap unnecessary have become popular (see page 19).

Climbing Shoes

Footwear is a complex subject. Climbing shoes for beginners do not need any particular shape, but they must fit well. This means they should fit as tightly as possible, without pinching the toes and making you want to rip them off after each climb. Extremely tight-fitting shoes have a noticible benefit only at more difficult climbs (see Table Page 200). Because slippers and many soft shoes with Velcro closures must be worn as a close fit, these are not suitable for beginners. With lace-up shoes, climbers can take small steps using less energy, and they fit the foot better (photo 4).

4

Slipper

Lace-up

Velcro

TIP: *The cheapest-fitting climbing shoe is usually the best for a beginner, because the first pair you use is quickly worn out from footwork mistakes.*

Safety Equipment

The HMS carabiner (which comes from a German term meaning half clove hitch belay; photo 5) is and remains the best to use with a belay device (see pages 35-47). It differs from the other locking carabiners by its typical pear shape.

5

Screw-locking

HMS

Spring-lock

Rock Climbing

6

7

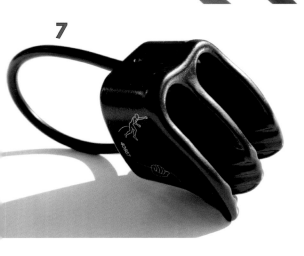

The still widely-used belay with a fixed Figure Eight abseil device (photo 6) will sooner or later be superseded by the tuber device (or ATC; photo 7), because the tuber has a higher braking force and there is less chance of mishandling (Albert, 2007a).

Assisted braking devices, such as GriGri and Cinch, are not suitable for beginners. If the belayer instinctively reaches for the belay device when a partner falls, the automatic brake mechanism may be disabled. In addition, assisted braking devices are expensive and require some practice when lowering a partner.

Chalk

Chalk (magnesium carbonate) binds the sweat on the hands and, thus, increases friction on steep slabs or rounded edges. For beginners, chalk is only recommended for those who tend to suffer from extremely sweaty hands. In quite a number of walls, only chalk balls are permitted since they release a smaller dose of powder and reduce the formation of dust. A completely dust-free alternative is liquid chalk (photo 8).

8

Climbing Ropes

Climbing ropes are already installed in the top roping sections of most indoor climbing walls. They are suspended from an anchor point and cover exactly the length of the route to be climbed. Both ends of the rope must reach to the floor, preferably with an excess of 1-2 m of rope at each end. Although, for the time being, the beginner does not need to worry about purchasing a rope, but he should nevertheless understand some of the characteristics about ropes. Climbing ropes are between 10 and 11 mm thick and have a breaking strain of at least 20 kN. More simply expressed, though not physically entirely correct, that means that the rope has a tensile strength of up to about 2,000 kg. The outer colored sheath of the rope is a protective mantle for the core but should still have no signs of damage. If the white core of the rope can be seen through the covering, the rope must not be used, and climbing wall management must be made immediately aware of it. Through frequent usage, the ropes become rough. Such ropes are still usable but are harder to handle. If this makes ensuring your partner's safety difficult, they should be replaced.

For setting up anchor points or more advanced climbing techniques in the sports wall, you need the following additional material.

Carabiners

Carabiners come with screw fastening or spring-lock fastening gates (photo 5). The most common carabiners are locking carabiners, with a locking mechanism to prevent unintentional opening. These are used, for example, for holding additional weight or the construction of rope anchor points. Due to their shape, regular locking carabiners are unsuitable for HMS, but HMS carabiners can serve the same purpose as locking carabiners.

Accessory/Prusik Cord

Accessory/Prusik cords are thin ropes with a diameter of 4-7 mm. Among other things, they are used for connecting additional weight. Their breaking strain—depending on the diameter—is between 3 and 10 kN. They are used mainly as knotted slings (photo 9).

Tape Slings

Tape slings are made of sewn webbing consisting of polyamide or Dyneema (photo 9). They come in different widths (10-30 mm) and lengths (30-240 cm). They have a breaking strain—like climbing ropes—of at least 20 kN. Slings are among the most relevant security-related equipment, and therefore must be inspected regularly for damage.

9

l = Tape slings

r = Belaying rope

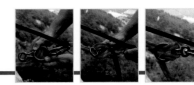 **Rock Climbing**

1.2 Fixing the Climbing Harness

Putting on the Harness

Before putting on the harness, it must first be properly laid out. This is often a challenge for inexperienced users, especially when the belt is twisted and the leg straps and loops must be sorted out. The following five steps explain the structure of a belt and help later to put it on correctly.

The climber takes the wide, usually padded, waist belt in both hands so that

- both leg loops hang down next to each other without any twists,
- the elasticized part of the leg loop is inside (toward the climber),
- the belay loop (connection between leg loops and waist strap) is facing forward, and
- adjustable leg straps and the leg loop buckles, if present, point forward so that they are outside the lower rings.

If a harness appears to be completely twisted, it is helpful to lay it on the ground and rearrange it there. Once staightened out, the harness is pulled on like a pair of trousers and fixed above the pelvic bones by tightening the buckle on the waist belt.

Equipment and Safety Techniques

ATTENTION: *The tongue on classic types of buckles has to be threaded back through the buckle (photos 10-12); otherwise it may not close tightly and hold properly, and the belt buckle could open under strain.*

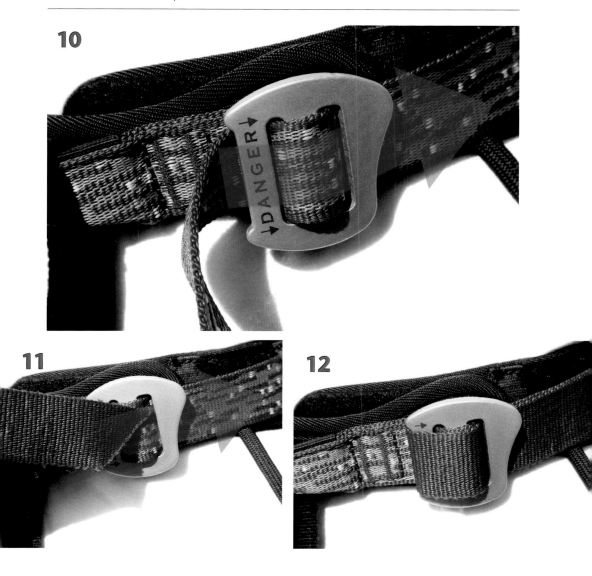

Speed Adjust buckles (see photo 3, page 11) only need to be pulled tight. They tighten by themselves, and the strap is stitched thickly at the end so that it is almost impossible that it will slip out freely.

On harnesses with adjustable leg loops, the buckles are tightened so that there is still room to push three to four fingers in between the leg and the loop. Thus, the leg loops sit as tight as the waist belt. Non-adjustable leg loops should sit similarly.

As mentioned earlier, smaller children up to about 8 years should use a full-body harness (photo 2, page 11). Due to the proportion of their head to the body, the body's center of gravity is located higher up on the body (in the area of the rib cage). The probability of falling head first is greater than with older children, adolescents, and adults and the danger is lessened by having a higher placed belay loop on the full-body harness.

ATTENTION: *The term seat harness can possibly lead to a dangerous misunderstanding: It must not be worn too low on the hips, but rather you must—as described above—be buckeled it up at the waist.*

Tying the Knot for the Tie-In to the Harness

There are two types of knots generally used to attach the harness to the climbing rope: the rethreaded Figure Eight knot, and the double bowline knot. We recommend the rethreaded Figure Eight knot, sometimes called double. It is the most commonly used tie-in knot, because it easy to learn. Tying the double bowline is more complicated than the Figure Eight and partner checks are harder to verify. This is why the Figure Eight has become popular for the tie-in to the harness for beginners. It can be practiced in advance at home, in the classroom, or at the climbing wall. In the following section, the two methods of tying the knot are illustrated, and the pictures make them easy to learn—for children and adults alike. The method of tying the knot is always described and illustrated for a right-handed person. The method for left-handed people is shown only in the photos and without a description.

First, measure out a roughly 1-m-long piece of rope to use for tying the knot (photo 13).

Hold the rope in the hands with the palms pointing toward your body. Hold the end of the rope in the right hand (photo 14). Form an eyelet loop by bending the right hand over so that the back of the right hand is pointing toward the body (photo 15).

NOTE: *In photos 14-35, the rope end is shown as a shortened version for clearness.*

The loop you have formed is a bight. Now bring the rope once round behind the bight and jump through into the bight (photos 16-18). The first part of the Figure Eight is now finished (photo 19).

NOTE: *In photos 14-35, the rope end is shown as a shortened version for clearness.*

Photos 20-25 illustrate the method for left-handed people.

NOTE: *In Photos 14-35, the rope end is shown as a shortened version for clearness.*

Another way of describing the first part is as follows: Measure out 1 m of rope (photo 13). The left hand holds the "doll's head". The right hand holds the rope end piece (photo 26). The "doll" has a sore throat, so we have to wrap a shawl around it by bringing the right hand between the body and the left hand clockwise round the doll's head (photos 27 and 28).

Because the doll is still crying, we put a dummy in its mouth (i.e., the end of the rope is put through the "doll's head" from the front; photos 29 and 30). The first part of the Figure Eight in this version is now finished (photo 31).

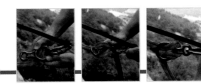
The method for left-handed people is illustrated in photos 32-36.

36

From here on in, the actions for the tie-in are the same for right- and left-handed people.

Now move the end of the rope alongside the run of the rope in the knot until it is doubled. Starting with the rope that comes from the belt, bring the rope round the whole knot like a train on the track until it comes out the other side again (photos 37-43).

Pull the knot tightly so that it is lying exactly on the belay loop (photo 44). The end of the rope must stick out from the double Figure Eight knot by at least a hand's length. If the run of the ropes is not exactly parallel, there is no danger; the rope will only be a little more difficult to release than if it were tied more cleanly.

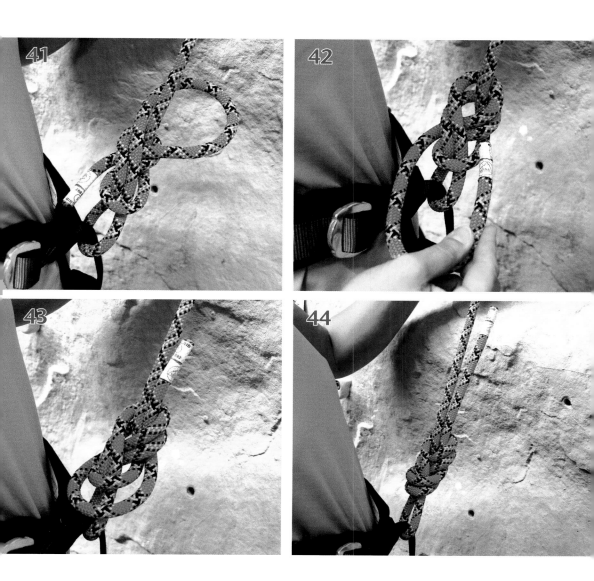

In order to undo the knot, it is recommended that you bend the knot backward and forward until the strains have loosened a little. You can then begin pulling the rope out of the knot.

At many indoor walls, climbers leave the first part of the Figure Eight knot in the rope after untying. It is advisable to remove the knot completely from the rope. This way, one learns the correct method of judging the optimum length of rope needed for tying and the correct method for tying the complete knot.

In many textbooks and in the harness manufacturer's safety instructions, it is recommended to do the tie-in through the eyelet on the waist band and the lower loop on the leg. This version of the tie-in has its advantages for advanced climbers. For beginners, we recommend doing the tie-in through the belay loop for clarity and easier handling. Both versions are safe.

TIP: *Every indoor climbing wall has old ropes as scrap, and sections can be cut from them and the ends can be sealed, using heat cutters or a soldering iron. If there are no harnesses available to practice on, any length of rope used must be at least long enough to wrap round your waist. Gymnastic ropes can also be used for practice.*

1.3   Securing Your Partner

In an ideal situation, both climbing partners are of similar weight. For advanced and very experienced climbers, it is acceptable for the climber to be 30-40% heavier than his belaying partner. Securing is done almost exclusively using the body (i.e. the belay device is attached to the harness; photo 45).

A fall is caught softer when the belay device is attached to the body than to an anchor point on the wall face (photo 103, page 60). An additional advantage is that the climber can vary his foothold, in order to free the run of the rope for the second climber, for example. In principle, the belay stand should be as close as possible to the wall face and close to the fall line from the anchor point. It is only at the start of a climb that the belayer may move a few meters sideways so that the other climber does not fall on top of him in the event of a slip, because...

ATTENTION: *...even when top roping, a fall into the rope over the first few meters can quite possibly be as far as 1-2 m!*

This is because the rope can stretch considerably during a fall, especially on long routes.

Example: On a 15-m route, after one has climbed 1 m, there is at least 29 m of rope between the lead climber and his securing partner. With an average rope stretch of 6-8% and an assumed weight of 176 lb (80 kg) (standard weight of a person) the impact of the fall results in an increased length of at least 2 m. This means that the climber will hit the ground even if the rope was held very tightly. Both climbers must watch out for this! The frequent complaint by the climber that the belayer was inattentive is completely unjustified in such a case.

While climbing, the belayer's attention must be solely on the lead climber and not on what is happening around him. An exception for this is during the last few meters when you are lowering your partner (see page 47).

TIP: *When top rope climbing, you should regularly practice deliberately planned falls first and unannounced falls later. This applies particularly to climbing partners with weight differences. The partners must learn to react quickly and correctly and come to trust each other.*

1.3.1 The HMS Belay Device

Despite many contrary opinions, tests repeatedly show the HMS carabiner as the belay device with the lowest failure rate (Trenkwalder, Schwiersch, Mersch & Stopper, 2005; Winter, 2000 and 2005). The advantages the HMS (German for **Ha**l**b**m**a**stwurf**s**icherung) lie in the low cost of materials, its versatility and above all in its **high braking force**. Even children can use them with relatively low hand effort to effect good security (Albert, 2007b). Disadvantages are that it causes more rope rub off when lowering and handling is more difficult with old and heavily worn ropes.

There are different ways to attach the rope to the HMS carabiner, which are described below for a right-handed person.

For indoor climbers top roping this is the easiest method: The HMS carabiner is clipped in with the lock on the left and the narrow side facing the belay loop of the harness, and the lock is screwed shut. Holding the end of the HMS in the right hand, you pull, with the left hand, a loop of rope upwards through the HMS carabiner. The ropes must not cross over each other (Photo 46). The end of the rope is then passed upwards through this loop (Photos 47-49).

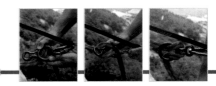

Rock Climbing

Photos 50-53 show the method for left-handed persons.

The following method can be used to attach the HMS knot at any point in the rope. This is always necessary when there is a lot of free rope behind the knot. Right-handed persons hold the climbing rope coming from the climber in both hands, so that the back of the hands point towards the climber (Photo 54). With the right hand, a loop of rope is laid over the left hand (Photo 55), which is then transferred into and held in the left hand (Photo 56). With the same motion (Photo 57) the right hand makes a second loop; imagine of a pretzel or a pair of glasses. In the correct method of attachment there is a vertical strand of rope in **front** and another vertical strand **behind** the horizontal piece of rope (Photo 58). You now close both of the "eyes of the pretzel" or "glasses" together like a book (Photos 59 and 60). Both "lenses" are now placed in the open HMS carabiner held in the belay loop of the harness without twisting it (Photos 61-63). This point is particularly important so that device is simple for a right-handed person to use. The HMS carabiner is now screwed shut.

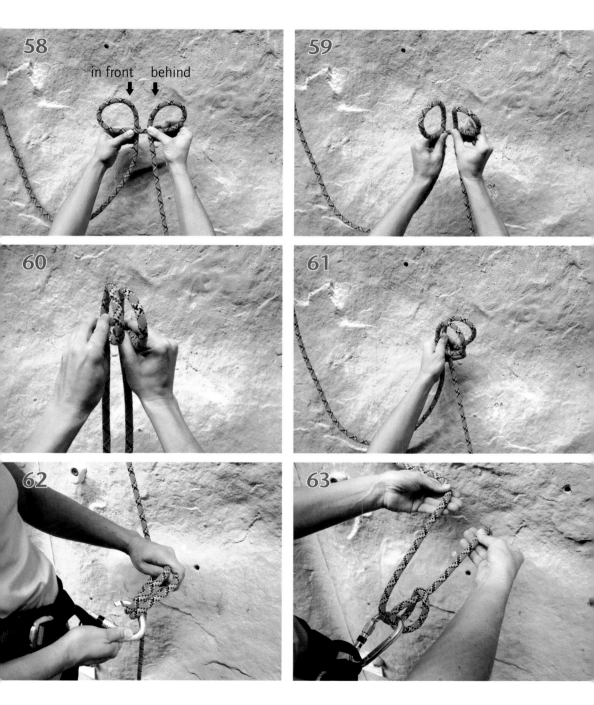

in front   behind

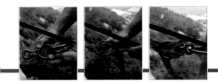

Rock Climbing

Photos 64-71 show the method of attachment for a left-handed person.

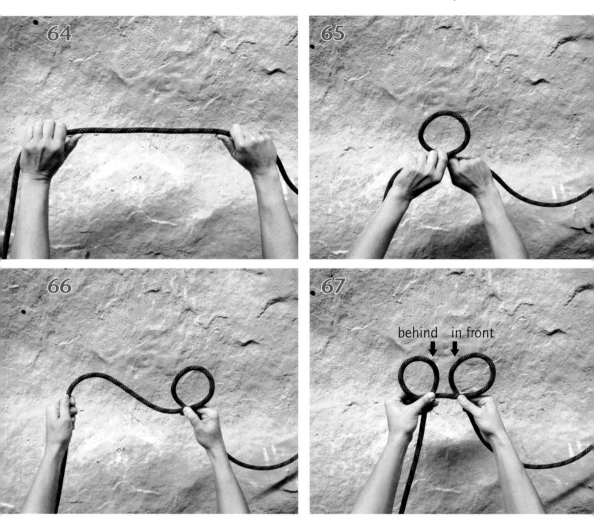

64

65

66

67

behind   in front

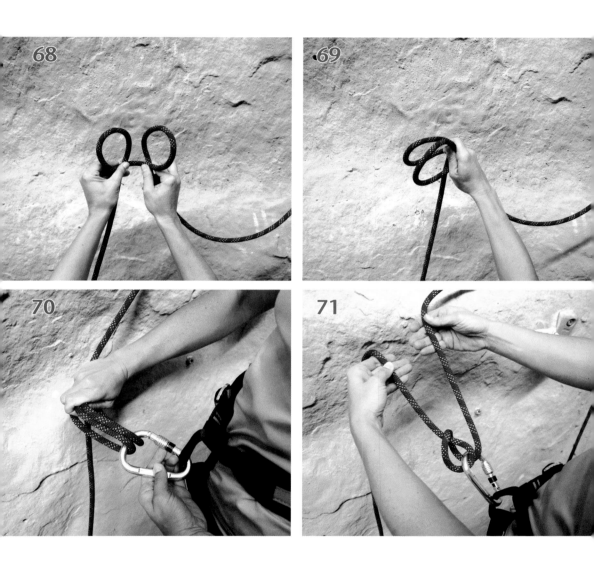

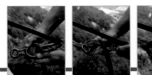

Following on from the methods described in a) or b), the way forward is: For right-handed people, hold the end of the rope in your right hand—this is the brake rope—and the top rope is held in the left hand (Photo 72).

Both hands are held at shoulder height above the HMS. This gives a good view of the arrangement. When alternately pulling on the brake rope or the top rope, the knot visibly twists around. This shows the difference between pulling in and giving out the rope.

Before the climber starts upwards, the rope is pulled tight by the belayer so that both feel the rope strain at the harness belt. This ensures that both partners are using the same rope and not accidentally using different ones. This principle also applies for securing with other belay devices.

Leading hand on the top rope

Brake hand on the brake rope

Before the serious part of the climb begins…

ATTENTION: *…always carry out a buddy check (see Page 55).*

When operating the HMS—as with all other belay devices also—never let go of the brake rope. Photos 72-77 show the process of securing when the partner begins to climb – in other words when rope has to be pulled in:

The leading hand pulls the rope tightly down to the HMS while the brake hand pulls the brake rope upwards from the HMS. The fingers point towards the body and the thumbs point upwards (Photos 73 and 74). The leading hand reaches down under the brake hand and takes hold of the brake rope (Photo 75) freeing the brake hand to reach down towards the HMS (Photo 76). The distance from the HMS should be at least one hand's breadth. The leading hand switches back upwards to hold the top rope (Photo 77) and pulls this—if necessary—back down tight to the HMS.

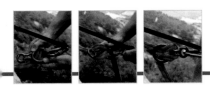

Photos 78-81 show the procedure for a left-handed person.

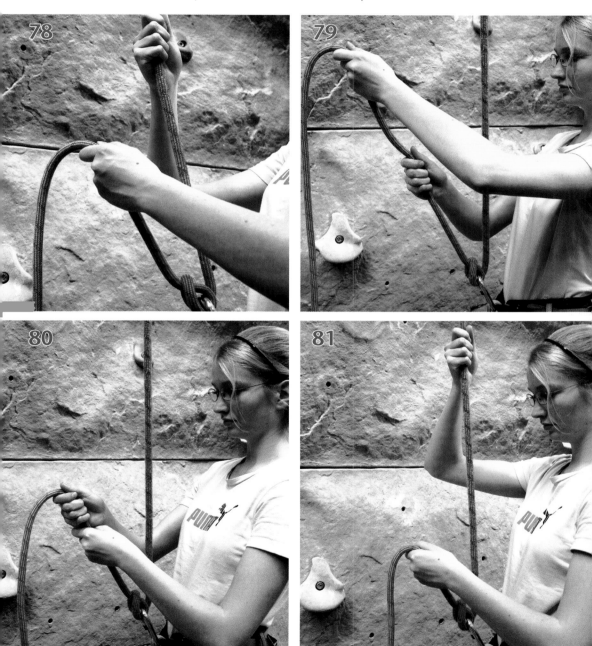

When climbing, beginners in particular like to have a really good "tight" rope. Too much of the "good" can however also have disadvantages: A particularly tightly drawn top rope can twist the HMS knot in the carabiner and block it. In this case the knot can no longer "turn" and it prevents rope being pulled in. Usually a short tug on the top rope suffices to get the knot free again. If this doesn't work, there are two further solutions:

- You can ask an 'experienced' climber who is standing by for help—or—
- You tell the climber to adopt a position as he would when preparing to be lowered (see Page 56). As the weight of the climber comes onto the rope and pulls it tight, the HMS knot twists into the correct position and is operable again. In both cases, the lead climber must be warned of the situation (call out his name and the command "Stop") so that he doesn't try to carry on climbing.

ATTENTION: *There should be no excessive slack rope between the climber and the belayer. If one is not careful when belaying, this can occur both above and below the leading hand (Photo 82). Both climbers must watch out for this. If the climber is moving rapidly, it can be difficult for the belayer to pull in the rope quickly enough. This is where appropriate communication between partners helps.*

When the climber has reached the top anchor point at the end of a route, lowering begins with the command "Take!" (see Page 56). The belayer transfers his leading hand to the brake rope so that now both hands hold the brake rope. After calling out the command "I've got you!", the belayer begins to lower the climber slowly down by giving the rope hand over hand through the carabiner. The rope must never be allowed to slip through the hands, even if you see this happening sometimes with others. A thin, new and smooth rope can easily cause burns to the belayer's hands as well as leading to a bumpy landing for the climber! Make sure that you always have one hand firmly on the brake rope. The belayer must keep his eye on the rope and not on his partner. The lead climber is only glanced at occasionally and—when necessary—made aware of any obstacles on his route. For example, this could be to warn him of any other climbers in the gym below him, who also have to be warned that you are lowering your climber.

TIP: *Beginners always use the HMS! Top rope and brake rope run always parallel and the hands are always at about shoulder height during the process and are thus well in view of the belayer.*

ATTENTION: *One hand holds firmly onto the brake rope so that—in the possible unexpected case of a fall by the lead climber—the rope doesn't slip through. The brake hand should be no closer than a hand's breadth above the HMS so that the hand doesn't become jammed in (it).*

1.3.2 The Tuber Belay Device

The tuber (also called ATC) is a belaying device that is becoming very popular particularly for top rope climbers. According to Britschgi (2004), the device is one of the simplest, uncompromising belay devices for one pitch climbs. It is easy to use and is a logical piece of equipment. Rope rub off is little when lowering. The disadvantages of the ATC over the HMS are in its lower average braking effect—particularly when pulling in the rope—and in a lack of visible control while operating it. Because of their lack of hand strength, children should always use the HMS.

Currently, the most functional ATC has two notches with ribbing (Photo 7 Page 14). This allows a very measured and at the same time, high braking effect in two different versions: when the rope runs through the notched side, the result is a high braking effect, when the rope runs through the flat side, you have normal braking.

Using the ATC: The rope is threaded into the ATC so that the leading rope is closest to the body and the brake rope points towards the wall. For right-handed people thread through the right-hand slot and for left-handers through the left slot. The rope is then placed together with the plastic-coated wire hanger of the ATC into the narrow side of the HMS carabiner with its longer side and the screw lock arrangement on the left for right-handed people (Photo 83) or with the lock to the right for left-handed persons (Photo 84). The arrangement is connected to the 'tie in' loop on the harness. The carabiner lock is then screwed shut.

For right-handed persons, the left hand is the leading hand. This hand holds the rope above the ATC leading up to the climber. The right hand is the brake hand and holds the rope always **below** the ATC (Photo 85).

Photos 86-91 show the process of the belay actions. After a partner check (see Page 55) and the start of the climb, the belayer pulls the top rope tight down to the ATC with the brake rope end lifted briefly to allow the rope to pull through the belay device. The brake hand is lifted for a fraction of a second above the ATC and is reflexively pushed back down again. This reflex "brake hand down" is important, because the braking effect is only achieved by this action. Then the brake hand slides down again in the direction of the ATC to the first position without releasing the brake rope.

85

Leading hand on the top rope

Brake hand on the brake rope

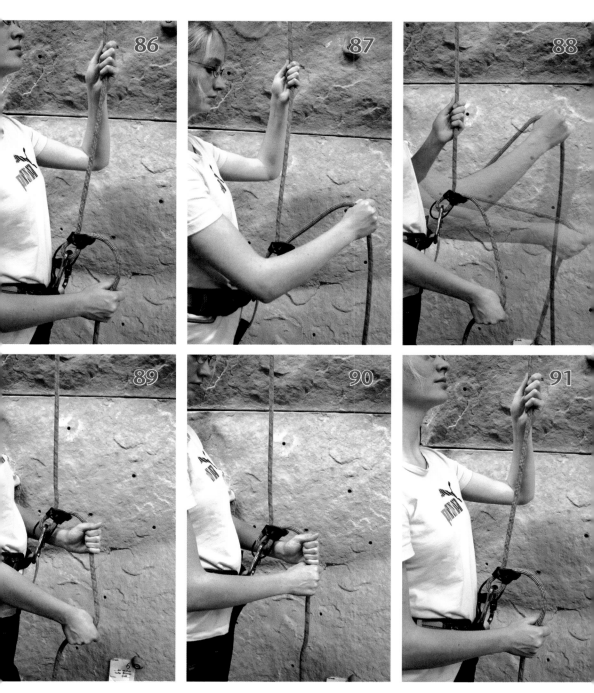

92

This is known as a loose-fit of the brake hand or as tunneling. Your brake hand is slightly open so that it can slip along the rope in the direction of the ATC. Thumb, index and middle fingers maintain contact with the rope (Photo 92).

Beginners in this belay method should—similar as for the HMS—keep hold of the brake cable when pulling and giving the rope. This guarantees that in all cases, one hand has a firm hold of the brake rope.

As with all belay devices, you should not tug the brake rope too sharply, because this makes the equipment difficult to operate. The brake rope end always runs in a slight bow down out of the ATC.

When the lead climber wants to come down again, the belayer calls out the command (see Page 56) and takes up the brake rope in both hands and lowers the partner down "hand to hand" until he is standing back on the ground again. The hand furthest away from the ATC maintains a firm hold on the brake rope well below the ATC. The hand closest to the ATC is opened so that the lower hand can feed rope into the ATC until both hands touch each other. The brake rope is now grabbed by the hand nearest the ATC again thus allowing the lower hand to be opened and move down to also grab the rope (Photos 93-95).

ATTENTION: *Particular care and attention is required when using new, smooth and thin ropes and when belaying heavier partners. Beginners tend not to 'tunnel', but bring the rope in "hand to hand" and feed it out in the same way. Even so, they also maintain a firm hold on the brake rope when using the ATC. Even if this appears awkward at first, safety comes first! There will be plenty of opportunities to relearn how to tunnel at a later date with regular climbing practice.*

1.3.3 The Fixed Figure Eight Belay Device

"The figure of eight turns out to be the belay device with which most handling errors occur" (Trenkwalder et al 2005). The result of this study is also in line with our personal experience. Therefore we have limited ourselves in the presentation of appropriate belay methods for beginners by covering only the HMS carabiner and tuber (ATC). If, nevertheless, a figure of eight belay device is used it must be the fixed type. The correct use of the fixed figure of eight is shown in Photo 96 for information.

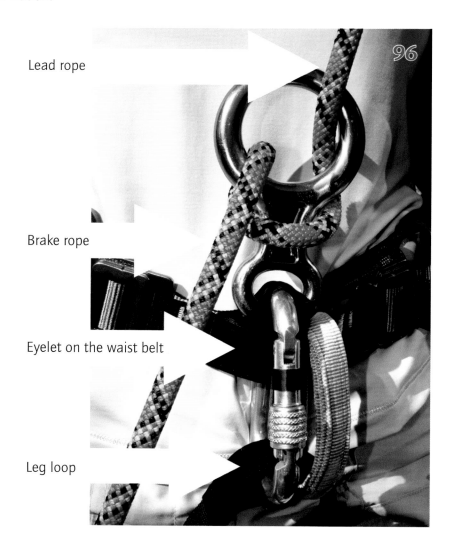

Lead rope

Brake rope

Eyelet on the waist belt

Leg loop

1.4   Partner 'Buddy' Check

The climber is roped up and the belayer has fed the rope into the belay device. Both check whether they are connected to the same rope and that it runs freely up to the top anchor point without any twists. A twisted rope does not mean that there is a safety risk, but means that it will have heavier wear. Photo 97 shows what partner checks must be made before the climber starts to climb the route:

- Is the harness correctly fastened both at the waist and the leg loops?
- Has the rope been fed correctly into the belay device?
- Is the carabiner closed correctly?
- Is the partner correctly tied in?

Partner's harness and knots OK?

Partner's harness and the belay device OK?

ATTENTION: *Don't start climbing without first doing a partner ('buddy') check! Studies have shown that 28% of climbing errors happen because the harness is fastened incorrectly and the rope is fed incorrectly into the belay device. These errors may be discovered if a thorough partner check is made beforehand (Mersch, Trenkwalder, Schwiersch & Stopper, 2005).*

1.5   Roping Commands and Lowering

When the climber reaches the anchor point (the top) or would like to be lowered back down, he calls out to his belaying partner loudly and clearly "Take!"

The belayer pulls in as much rope as possible and then also grasps the brake rope with his leading hand. His preparedness to take the weight of his partner is signaled by him calling: "I've got you!" or "Belay on!" Then, the climber puts his weight on his harness and loosens his hand grips (Photos 98-100) and replies "Ready to be lowered!" This is the most exciting moment for beginners when climbing.

His body weight is now hanging on the rope being held by his partner. The legs are almost fully stretched out and feet spread out roughly shoulder-width apart. The soles of the feet push against the wall (Photo 101). On the command "Ready to be lowered!" from the climber, the belayer feeds the rope through the belay device "hand over hand" (HMS) or "hand to hand" (ATC) until the climber is back on the ground. His attention is first and foremost on the operation of the belay device, the brake rope and on a slow and steady descent, rather than on the climber.

ATTENTION: *If the belayer is lighter than the climber then after the command "Take!", the belayer settles down into a half squat in order to lower his centre of gravity. He always positions himself close to the wall and the fall line below the anchor point.*

Back-Up Safety

When practicing climbing with school classes, it is best to form teams of three. The third person functions as back-up safety. This also reduces the number of teams, increasing the manageability of the teams and safety in the class. The back-up holds the climbing rope about 1-1.5 m behind the belayer (photo 102). In other words, he pulls in as much rope as he can without hindering the belayer. On the other hand, should the belayer make a serious mistake, he is there to ensure the climber doesn't tumble down to the ground.

In practice, there should always be a little slack rope between the back-up and the belayer. If the rope is held too tightly, then the belayer might leave it to the back-up to belay, and the situation would become unclear. If there is too much slack, then the actions by the back-up would not make much sense.

ATTENTION: *Particularly with children and adolescents, there is a danger that chatter begins between the back-up and the belayer who will therefore become less attentive. The tasks and individual responsibilities of belayer and back-up must be laid down clearly!*

TIP: *The back-up can be best compared to an airbag in an automobile: You don't see it, you don't hear it, but when you need it, it is there!*

1.6 Securing Using a Fixed Point or a Counterweight

103

If there is a large difference between the weight of the climber pairs, in some climbing gyms you will find it advantageous to belay from a fixed point, normally a bolt in the wall (Photo 103). For this only the HMS can be used, as it is very difficult and complicated to belay correctly from a fixed point using an ATC or Figure Eight. The fixed points are generally mounted low, so that to operate the belay device correctly (brake rope downwards) the belayer must continually stoop or crouch.

ATTENTION: *Belaying using a fixed point is less dynamic than using the body and therefore, for the climber in the case of a fall, very much harder.*

Where there are no fixed points close to ground level on the wall, in many gyms you will find additional weights (large stones, steel blocks, sandbags etc.,) to which the belayer can rope onto so that he is not pulled off the ground by the weight of the partner. The attachment to the additional weight is made using a rope loop or a webbing loop with a carabiner on the belay loop (Photo 104).

Alternatively, a sling around the waist belt can be used. The attachment to the fixed point then runs behind the body (Photo 105). New climbing harness models have a special loop specifically for use on such a loading (breaking load at least 5 kN) and they are appropriately designed for this kind of belay work.

ATTENTION: *Attachment to an additional weight must not be done using an equipment loop on the harness. These are only used for carrying equipment and are not designed for other types of work in the event of a fall.*

2　Climbing Techniques

106

In sport, the term 'technique' implies the ability to carry out a movement safely and effectively according to an ideal method. In climbing, unlike other sports such as gymnastics, there are no laid down rules from a textbook. Also the equipment (i.e., the wall) is not standardized. Quite the opposite—it is very variable. Climbing is a sport characterized by the freedom of the movements you carry out, and there are numerous ways of carrying out a climb.

Moreover, the methods available are not equally effective for all climbers because of the different individual conditions: body size and leverage capability as well as strength and flexibility all play a part in the selection of methods used to complete the task. So there can be many different methods for the same route and all can achieve the goal. Beginners usually lack an overview over the different techniques and hence don't see the full range of possibilities. They mainly use a frontal climbing position (Photo 106) and this brings one to one's limit, because the next grip or step may be out of sight.

When we speak about climbing techniques in the following passages, we are referring to the series of movement principles that ease the way to the top.

For the first contact with the climbing wall there should be no special guidelines and rules. The first meters of climbing are usually exciting, so that you can focus more on the feeling and experience rather than on carrying out specific techniques. The sense of achievement, of climbing up high and, with luck, possibly reaching the end of the climb is quite possible without any special training.

Only when the climber feels safe and has learned to trust his partner and master the variety of essential, safety-relevant basic information can the technical aspects of the sport be brought into play. These should help him to climb to good heights using less energy and aid in coping with more difficult routes.

The fundamental objective for the beginner should always be the development of a total body awareness. Typical climbing movement patterns can then be recognized, for example controlling the body's center of gravity and balance.

2.1 Changing the Center of Gravity of the Body and Balance Control

The body's center of gravity in young people (standing) and adults is located roughly between the navel and lumbar part of the spine. Its location is changed with every movement. For the retention of balance, it is crucial that the body maintains the line of gravity (vertical line from center of gravity of a body within the base of support with minimal postural sway—in other words the body's center of gravity must always be above the spread of the standing posture. On inclined and vertical climbing walls this is not particularly difficult. However, on overhangs or roofs one needs greater mobility and arm strength to keep the body on the wall. The more the body's center of gravity is centrally above the standing posture, the more stable the equilibrium.

Almost all climbing movements begin with a shift of the body's center of gravity. The weight of the body normally rests on both legs when standing. When preparing to move a leg, the body weight shifts over the leg on which you will be standing. All the weight is on the one foot so that the climber stands on one leg.

Unencumbered, the other foot can now step sideways. If the shift of the hips in the transfer of the weight is more pronounced, less arm strength will be required and the whole movement will be more controlled. This type of movement, namely freeing a foot for the next step is quite normal for climbers. Further movement is a repeat of taking the next step—freeing the one leg by shifting the body center of gravity in the direction of the climb (Photos 107-114).

BASIC EXERCISE

A partner goes in slow motion round the indoor climbing gym. On a command, he has to stop immediately and try—without losing balance—to remain still. He will only be able to do this if one foot is placed freely down first and then the weight of the body is moved slowly onto this leg. When the whole body weight is resting on that leg, the rear foot can be lifted. Once the exercise is successful on level ground, it can be tried on a staircase.

TIP: *When climbing every beginner should keep asking himself: "Is my balance correct?" "Is the body center of gravity over the stepping foot?" "Can I take the next step freely?"*

107

108

109

110

2.2   Footwork

Good footwork techniques are the key to an effective style of climbing. Therefore, we will cover these before speaking about grip techniques. You will be able to climb more successfully standing on your feet rather than hanging by the arms! If you want to climb using less energy then you must learn good footwork. The basis of footwork is being able to stand correctly. Only when you have a good standing position can you employ your grip techniques well.

Even the smallest of steps must be precisely and thoroughly carried out so that your foot has a firm base. Small steps using the edge of the shoe are done on the inside of the foot (Photo 115). This gives you a good hold.

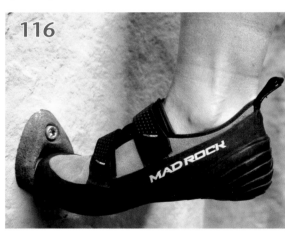

In pockets and sharp protrusions you use the toes (Photo 116). In conjunction with the backstepping technique (see Page 73 et seq) your weight is placed on the outer edge of the foot (Photo 117). For all footwork techniques, the sole of the shoe is always used in a horizontal plane.

This is different on steep inclines where friction is used when stepping (Photo 118). Here the heel is lowered slightly so that the entire forefoot touches the wall thus allowing more sole area to be used. This creates more friction and therefore more grip.

In the advanced stages of the techniques, the top of the toe and the heel are used in order to gain a more favorable body position. The usage of the toes is called **'toe-hooking'** and the use of the heel **'heel hooking'**.

For clean and energy-saving techniques in footwork, 'eye-foot-coordination' is essential. By this we mean keeping almost constant control and view of the unweighted foot until the next step is carried out.

BASIC EXERCISE:

Climb up a slightly inclining wall without using the hands. Use only stepping and shifting the body's center of gravity. If the arms are used to keep your balance, only use them under head height to hold onto the wall, so that feet, not the arms do the work.

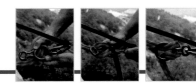
2.3 Using Handholds and Grips

Almost subconsciously, a beginner will focus far more on the hands than on a good grip with the feet. Therefore, while he is climbing he will concentrate on searching for the next best handhold. As a result he loses much time and energy; to increase efficiency, make sure you properly use handholds even if they are not perfect. The aim is to place the proper hold on whatever is available.

Since on inclines and vertical beginner routes the hands primarily serve to safeguard against the body tipping backwards, you should always try to maintain the grip only as firmly as necessary. This "soft gripping" saves strength and provides for proper footwork techniques.

All handholds can be used irrespective of whether the strain is in a downwards, upwards or sideways direction. According to this they are called top-, undercling- or sidepull-grips. You should always try to place as many fingers as possible on the climbing handhold. If the handhold is very small or shaped so that only little space exists, it may be in order to have the fingers crossed over each other—e.g., the thumb over the index finger or the middle index finger crossed over the ring finger. Also it is ok to have one hand over the other if there is no alternative handhold available in reach. Gripping a handhold from underneath (undercling) or from its side (side pull) feels, at first, very unusual and gives little confidence that all will be well. However, once you learn to bring the body's center of gravity up higher or even above the handhold when gripping an undercling handhold (Photo 119), then a well stretched-out arm will give you a good and energy-saving holding point. Side pull handholds (Photo 120) will be easier to hold onto when the body's center of gravity is well to one side as you lean away from the hold.

When employing a 'pinch' type handhold (Photo 121), the fingers are placed on the side of the handhold and the thumb grips the opposite side as a counterbalance.

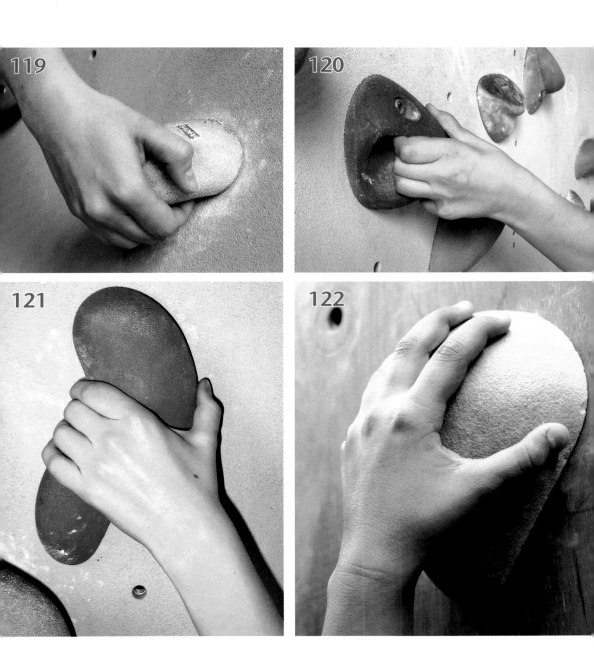

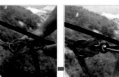

In order to maximize friction as far as possible when gripping, small protrusions or flat dimples must have a lot of friction to be effective (Photo 122). You must have a lot of contact with the fingers and the palm of the hand as you bear down on the dimple using the effect of friction (sometimes called 'palming'). This is easier if the forearm is rested on the wall underneath the handhold.

Beginners tend to concentrate the search for the next handhold mostly upwards. When a route is difficult, there is less likelihood that this will always be successful. A glance downwards will often reveal the next handhold available—a prop (sometimes called a 'volume') (Photo 123). Almost all good handholds can also be used as supporting 'prop' grips. This relieves the strain on the arms and at the same time takes the weight off the foot that is needed to take the next step higher.

Every prop grip used will improve your climbing abilities and technique.

TIP: *Grip the handhold only with the amount of strength needed. Glance downwards to see if there is a 'volume' hold that can help you out.*

2.4   'Backstep' Techniques

Backstepping, a few years ago a still unusual method of climbing and used only by experienced climbers, has become a basic style of climbing. This was the result of the boom in indoor climbing, because on artificial walls this style offered many more alternatives of movement beyond the favored frontal method preferred by beginners. The advantages of this style are the energy saving closeness of the body's center of gravity to the wall and the better reach needed to cover big distances between handholds.

In its description, the movement sounds complicated, but, in practice it is easy to understand using Photos 124-128: In the frontal position, you stand with shoulders and pelvis parallel to the wall. The right hand is holding onto a sideways handhold at head or shoulder height. You then turn the body around its longitudinal axis and bring the left shoulder forwards towards the wall. The right shoulder is pulled backwards away from the wall. At the same time, you bring the outside of the left foot across underneath the right hand and then bring the right foot up above the left foot. To do this you push the left leg through between the wall and right leg. The right foot must usually be turned in slightly onto the ball of the big toe.

To save energy, the right arm remains stretched out fully all the time. Now, the right foot is placed to the right of the right hand and the left foot. The right foot must not necessarily be placed into a foothold, but rather can be freely rested against the wall. The body has now completed a 90° turn through its longitudinal axis. Shoulder and pelvis are at right angles to the wall. In this phase of stabilization, the climber builds up a high tension in the body and can now— by extending the left leg—reach out to quite a distance with the left hand.

2.6 Chimneying and Jamming Techniques

Chimneying and jamming techniques can be used usefully where there are few handholds in passages such as dihedrals, chimneys and wide cracks. They help to save strength just like in backstepping. This technique is basically essential for a smooth and effortless climb. Due to the large space between the spread of the legs, often both hands can be freed from the handholds, thus relieving the strain on the arm muscles. The strong pressure exerted on the soles of the shoes in the spread leg position, makes it possible to use less favorable footholds, as well as steep inclines, to carry on climbing.

The climbing movement starts by supporting yourself with one hand about waist level. The foot on the same side is thereby freed and can be placed on a higher foothold. The other hand repeats this action correspondingly for a further step. Now, by stretching both legs you can gain height. Irrespective of what handholds are available; the hand that is not supporting is held either above the head and takes no strain, or is simply holding on (Photos 135-138).

Feeling insecure, beginners tend not to take advantage of using a propping handhold and try to use handholds to pull up on in places relatively too high for them, and this requires disproportionately more effort for further climbing.

ATTENTION: *The large spread of the legs can cause strain, cramp and injury to the muscles in a person who makes little use of the movements involving the hips and flexibility of the legs and this will hamper a climb. Warm-ups and stretching as well as regular exercises to improve flexibility can solve this problem relatively quickly.*

2.7   Layback Technique

The layback technique (also called "Dülfer technique" Photos 139-144) is an exceptional method in climbing. Here, the body's center of gravity is deliberately not placed over the feet but is rather held away from this line. You should use a counter pressure between the hands and the feet. This technique is very demanding and requires a lot of hand and body strength. It is good for use in chimneys, corners and on cracks.

Because of the large degree of opposing counter pressure required, the arms should be stretched out to cover as large an area as possible, as well as move quickly when used. The legs are kept slightly bent. The counter pressure will be higher the nearer the hands are to the feet.

For the beginner, this technique is less important, because in indoor climbing gyms rarely offer any good routes or passages where the layback technique can be used.

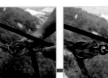

2.8   Problems and Solutions

A major problem for beginners on the first visit to an indoor climbing gym is when, after climbing only a few times, he gets "blow up arms". The relatively small muscle groups of the lower arms respond on the new strains with rapid fatigue. To counteract this, he should call on three basic climbing rules:

"Feet Before Hands" or "Climb—Do Not Pull Yourself Up"!

The main emphasis lies on the correct choice and effort placed on a foothold step and not on the search for the closest really good handhold.

BASIC EXERCISES:

- Climb a simple, familiar route using a rule of only using handholds below eye level.
- Climb, wearing a cap with the peak dragged as low as possible so that even when looking upwards you can only see handholds in front of you or below you.
- Climb a slightly inclining wall face wearing gloves—even better 'mittens'. Alternatively, you can put your hands into a pair of shoes for the same effect.
- Climb just with one hand, the other is pushed into the back of the harness.

TIP: *All the basic exercises can be used in several ways to improve climbing techniques and can be easily used to do warm-up exercises.*

Pay Attention to Shifting the Body's Center of Gravity!

You can only ease the strain somewhat on your arms by doing this correctly. The unweighted leg can then be placed correctly on the next step.

BASIC EXERCISES:

- A so-called nylon runner (webbed loop sling 60 or 80 cm) is attached to the center of the harness at the back. The sling is weighted down with a carabiner. When climbing a simple route, by shifting the body's center of gravity, the sling must swing out until it is over the loaded leg before the other foot is lifted.
- Climb an incline:
  - Without using your hands.
  - Using only one hand.
  - By using only prop grip/mantling handholds.

All the basic exercises in A) above are also good for practicing to shift your center of gravity.

Soft Hands!

Most of the time, beginners grasp hold of handholds as if they wanted to squeeze every last drop out of an already dry sponge. This is quite understandable, because at first they have a fear of falling. However, as soon as you trust your partner and are able to maintain a firm foothold using the climbing shoes, you have to learn to grasp handholds only as firmly as it needs to prevent one falling away from the wall. The idea of "caressing" the handholds can be a good help.

BASIC EXERCISES:

- Climb a simple route:
  - Wearing gloves (see above).
  - Only using the middle and ring finger.
  - Only using the middle finger.
  - Treating the handhold as a raw egg.

A further problem is the so-called **'barn-dooring'**. This occurs whenever the body's center of gravity is clearly too near the axis of the foot and handholds.

Every climber knows this problem. It is not possible to let go of a handhold without the body swinging away from the wall like a door opening. As no other alternative appears to be there, the beginner tries to resolve the problem by pulling up on the handhold and grabbing upwards. If he reaches the next handhold he is lucky, but—in so doing has used a lot of energy. If the handhold is a poor one, then he has had bad luck and swings away from the wall and thus loses a stabile body position from where to test the next handhold.

The best way to counter this problem is to practice close to the ground (bouldering). The girl climber in Photo 145 has the weight of her body on the left hand and the left foot. When she wants to reach a handhold with her right hand, her body will tip to the left and she will swing out like a door (Photos 146 and 147).

There are several options to choose from in order to stabilize the climbing position and continue climbing:

- The right leg is brought across and behind the left leg and the tip of the foot is against the wall (Photo 148). The right hand can now reach out further for a handhold from this position (Photo 149) and then the right foot can be placed down on a foothold again (Photo 150).

- In combination with a twist of the body, the right foot is pushed between the wall and the body and the tip of the toe is pressed against the wall (Photo 151). From here, you can now reach out for a handhold (Photo 152). Once the handhold is in the hand, you turn the body back again and continue placing the foot on the foothold (Photo 153).
- The climber then tries to toe-hook or heel hook onto a foothold or edge using his instep or the heel.
- A changeover of footholds allows you to place the right foot further to the right.

151

152

- Climb back and start again using the backstepping technique by placing the outside of the left foot on the former foothold to the right. The right foot is stretched out away and placed on the wall.

With more practice, you will get a good feel for your body position and be able to recognize whether the body is stabilized or not from the selection of footholds you make. This means that the next step is done either with the instep of the right foot or with the left foot turned so you use the outside of that foot.

153

2.9   Falling

Almost every beginner is afraid of falling. He therefore tends to abort a climb at a difficult point rather than risking a fall, even if he knows that he is secured by a tight rope. Nevertheless, all beginners will soon have sudden falls due to lack of experience with climbing techniques. If these falls are sudden they are usually harmless. But beginners with no experience of falls who feel an impending fall at the very last moment will react instinctively to prevent it. Such reflexes involve a high risk of injury. Climbers can avoid this risk by actively influencing and thereby controlling a fall. The belayer, too, must learn to stay active and alert all the time and stop a fall appropriately.

Systematic fall training on a regular basis is recommended to automate quick and correct responses in climbers and belayers likewise.

The terrain for fall training should meet the following criteria:

- The climbing wall must be at least vertical, preferably with a slight overhang.
- It should not be too short; the fall is softer and therefore more comfortable for both the more rope is left between climber and belayer.
- The fall area must not contain any obstacles.
- The danger of a fall to the ground must be excluded, i.e. prior to the fall the climber's feet should be at least 4 to 5 m above ground.
- The danger of a collision with the belayer or another climber must be excluded.
- The belayer must have a level and obstacle-free terrain.

2.9.1 Fall Training Exercises

The following three steps make sense in fall training:

- The climber leaves his static position on the wall without calling out the command "take". He releases both grips simultaneously, slightly pressing himself back with his feet. The upper body remains upright, legs are slightly bent and stretched forward to absorb wall contact.
- The climber is let down for 2 to 3 m, climbs again and now releases both hands during the movement, i.e. he touches the target hold but does not grasp it.
- The same as 2., whereby the climbing movement towards the target hold is carried out far more dynamically with a strong leg impulse, almost like a jump.

In all three steps, the belayer performs the "braking reflex", i.e. swiftly grasps the brake rope with his guide hand as soon as he notices or anticipates the fall.

In no case should a wide fall be practiced in combination with much slack rope and a blocked braking unit. Despite the slack the fall will be very hard and the climber can be harmed when colliding with the wall. The impact force on the belayer will be unpleasant as well. Ideally the belayer—as soon as he senses the fall—feeds rope into the braking unit to brake the impact of the fall. This rather unusual response, unusual since the obvious reflex in a fall is to "shut down", should be taught in a climbing course and practiced repeatedly to make it automatic.

A belayer who secures a partner of equal or even higher weight must expect to be lifted somewhat from the ground if the partner falls. He should be prepared for this effect and do it actively rather than let himself be surprised by it. If he is pulled up towards the wall he, too, must stretch out his legs in front to absorb a possible impact with his feet. If the climber is considerably lighter than the partner, the belayer must brake the fall softly in any case, which means he must actively feed rope into the braking unit at the end of the fall and move towards the falling climber.

Systematic fall training helps to reduce fears of falling. The advantage is that the beginner will be more decisive and less hesitant at difficult points. He will be more willing to experiment, and develop more self-confidence and a more fluid style. In this way he saves strength and copes with difficult routes more successfully. Beginners who after some fall training exercises believe to have mastered their fears should repeat fall training on a regular basis.

TIP: *Some experts advise against gripping the rope at the roping-up knot in a fall, to avoid injuries. But for insecure climbers this grip is a tremendous psychological relief and helps to stabilize the position of the upper body. Nevertheless, you should also practice falls without gripping the rope. In case of a wide fall, tense abdominal muscles help to stabilize the upper body.*

Please note: First experience with falls should always be gained in a climbing course under expert supervision.

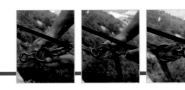

154

3 Equipment and Safety Techniques Outdoor

3.1. Material

155

Rope sack and lead-climbing equipment

The following equipment is essential for rock climbing:

- Climbing rope
- Harness
- Climbing shoes
- Climbing helmet
- Belay device (HMS carabiner or tuber with an HMS carabiner)
- Locking carabiner
- Quickdraws
- Tape slings
- Self-securing slings
- Prusik loops
- Information on the region and area to be climbed
- First Aid kit
- Chalk bag—if required

You should not go off and buy a complete set of equipment for your first climbing session on the rock. For a beginner with the right climbing partner, the indoor gym set of equipment (shoes, belt, and belay device) is perfectly sufficient. Additional equipment is usually available from most course organizers. After experiencing a few climbs, you will be in a better position to judge what is really necessary and what you prefer.

All pieces of equipment are subject to special standard ratings (EN, CE, UIAA required for safety) and must bear the appropriate rating abbreviation on the items.

TIP: *For your own safety, you should always obtain good advice from a specialty store, experienced rock climbers, or a qualified course leader before you ask for climbing equipment as a present. Safety equipment is usually excluded from exchange. Be careful when buying used lead-climbing equipment. Faults in ropes and carabiners are rarely detectable by the untrained eye.*

Climbing Rope

The own climbing rope is the principal piece of equipment for any outdoor climber. The rope is made in a "Kernmantel", or core sheath construction (i.e., it consists of a core inside hundreds of braided, spun, and woven nylon threads and a woven covering). Opinions vary about the optimal length of a climbing rope. For many years, the 50-m length was sold almost exclusively. This length, however, is too long for many climbing gardens in Germany, where climbs trend to be only 10-15-m high; here a 25-35-m length rope would be perfectly adequate. In Southern Europe, on the other hand, a 50-m rope will not suffice as many climbing routes exceed 30 m. In regions like these, the standard length is 60 or even 70 m.

Choosing the correct rope diameter is just as important. Lately, ropes have become thinner and lighter. This is particularly noticeable when negotiating long, vertical or overhanging routes. The weight on the harness feels considerably lighter. However, due to the thin covering mantle, thin ropes have a shorter lifespan and have less braking effect when used with an HMS belay. Thicker ropes are more robust, but are not as smooth after extended use and do not feed as well through belay devices.

Basically there are two types of rope:

- Ropes that are used only as a single strand are called single ropes. They have a diameter of 9-11 mm (see Photo 156).

- Ropes that are used as a double rope (as a pair) are called half ropes or twin ropes. These are usually made with a diameter of 7.5–9 mm (see Photo 156). They are impregnated and thus considerably more expensive, and are only necessary in Alpine regions and on mountain climbs where both rock and ice is encountered.

Lifespan: Ropes used in climbing gardens and in well-prepared sport-climbing routes are practically indestructible (Schubert, 2011). The possibility that a rope will break exists only under certain extreme conditions in mountainous regions (for example, when a fall occurs when the rope runs over a sharp edge). By using a double rope, this risk is minimized.

Rock Climbing

Rope manufacturers recommend that ropes in regular use—used more than once a week—should be replaced after one year at the latest. Safety tests carried out by the German Alpine Club (DAV), however, have shown that the lifespan of a rope—as long as it shows no sign of wear and tear or has not been stretched over sharp edges—is far longer than data stated by the manufacturers. The lifespan of a rope mostly depends on whether it has been used mainly for lead climbing and rappelling, or whether the rope was frequently used for top-roping and lowering of climbers: Top-roping and lowering are real "rope-killers."

A rope that had to withstand several long falls or on which the fiber mantle jacket has begun to come apart should not be used for lead climbing.

A rope should be changed when

- the rope mantle is damaged and the core is visible;
- the amount of use has abraded the rope so that it has become difficult to clip into belay devices;
- damage to the core can be felt through the mantle; or
- the rope has been in contact with chemicals or acid.

The use of a rope bag (see Photo 155) protects the rope from dirt and small grit particles and lengthens its lifespan considerably.

TIP: *An inexpensive single rope is usually the preferred choice for outdoor beginners. Its diameter should not be less than 9.8 mm and no more than 10.3 mm. If your local climbing crags are normally between 10- and 15-m high, a 25-3 m long rope will suffice. When the long anticipated climbing holiday in Southern Europe or other high mountain regions is at last realized, then this is the time for a 60-70 m rope.*

Consider purchasing two half ropes or a double rope only after years of experience in multi-pitch routes, or when taking up Alpine climbing. The numerous, well-appropriated 2-4 pitch routes in many climbing regions of Southern Europe or North America will give you many thrilling years of climbing.

156

Single rope   Twin/double rope

Climbing Harness

In sports climbing, climbers almost always use the seat harness (see Photo 157) well-known from the climbing gym. A full-body harnesses or the combination of a chest and seat harness (see Photo 158) is a sensible choice on longer Alpine routes with a heavy backpack or when there is an extreme risk of falling. For climbing in sports-climbing areas and climbing gardens—as described in this book—tying into a seat harness is perfectly sufficient. Climbing harnesses wear out much quicker when climbing outdoors rather than in the gym. The harness is stressed more when the belayer is tied into the rope and the belay anchor as well, and the belay loop must be checked regularly for damage. Adjustable leg loops are recommended when the temperature demands a change of clothing. Four gear loops, to which you can attach your climbing equipment so that it is east to get to, are also recommended.

157

One-sided overhand knot

158

One-sided overhand knot
(2 x)

Chest and seat harness with a strap connection

Climbing Shoes

When first beginning outdoor climbing, the shoes used in the gym are quite suitable. Outdoors, you should put on your shoes just before the climb and take them off immediately afterward. Otherwise, the soles will become dirty and will not stick well to footholds, and they will wear out considerably faster.

Climbing Helmet

We strongly recommend that you always wear a climbing helmet, even when the "experts" are climbing "topless," so-to-speak. Especially in easy, well prepared beginner routes, there are often rocks lying in larger footholds and on terrace or strip sections, and these can be dislodged by climbers or the movement of the rope. Thus, both the climber and the belayer should wear a helmet.

Belay Devices

There is a wide variety of products sold as belay devices that all have different and multiple uses, and this variety poses a noticeable problem. When you handle one belay device correctly but use the same procedure for a different make, this can lead to dangerous situations (Würtl, 2009). Many of the safe, good devices used in the gym have disadvantages when climbing outdoors. They conceal risks or may even be completely useless for protection of the follow-on climber (see Page 113). Because of its wide-use spectrum, the best choice for both indoor and outdoor climbing is the HMS carabiner. It is the most versatile belay device, and Walter Würtl (2009) calls it "the classic piece of equipment that is absolutely essential for use by climbing beginners as well as connoisseurs and experts in Alpine climbing alike." The only disadvantage is high rope wear, but this can be alleviated somewhat by rappelling rather than lowering down a climber (see Page 140 ff.).

Nevertheless, if you want to use a tuber device for the follow-on climb, you will have to use a plate (Photo 159). This is a belay device which is specially constructed with an eyelet for the belay of the follow-on climber (e.g., ATC Guide, Reverso).

Eyelet for follow-on climber protection

159

Sticht plate

However, the use of a plate demands practice and concentration in its handling— as some of the near-miss falls suffered by some very experienced climbers show (Mailänder, 2010; Zack, 2010). As a result, these devices are not recommended for the beginner.

We also do not recommend semi-automatic belay devices (e.g., GriGri, Cinch, Zap-o-Mat, Eddy, Sum, etc.) for outdoor beginners. For protection when lead climbing and steady lowering particularly, they require a lot of practice and can lead to risky handling; besides, they are very expensive.

Figure Eight belay   Plate   Tuber

Rappelling Devices

The choice of rappelling devices depends on the belay device used for the lead climb. If one uses the HMS carabiner exclusively, the Figure Eight is recommended for rappelling. Its advantage over the tuber is that the rope is more easily and faster attached to the rappelling device. If, however, the belay was done with a double-slotted tuber or a plate device, these can also be used for rappelling (Photo 160).

CAUTION: *Tubers with only one slot are not suitable for rappelling.*

Locking Carabiner

Besides the HMS carabiner that is necessary for the HMS belay or for belaying with a tuber, at least two additional locking carabiners are needed for rock climbing, for the anchor sling and the Prusik loop (Photo 161). A second HMS is also useful, especially on multi-pitch routes,

Locking carabiner

HMS carabiner

Quickdraws

During the ascent, the lead climber is protected by clipping in the rope to existing bolts or anchor points on the rock face. This is done with quickdraw slings (Photo 162).

A quickdraw has two different-sized loops sewn into it, with a carabiner clipped into both. During the climb, the carabiner in the larger loop—usually a straight-gate or a wire-gate carabiner—is clipped into the bolt. The smaller loop is then clipped to the rope, either with a spring-loaded wire gate or of a wire-gate type carabiner.

The number of quickdraws needed depends on the number of bolts on the climbing route. This information can be found in the guide for the particular climbing area. Normally, 10-12 quickdraws should be sufficient.

Slings and Prusik Loops

For securing yourself at a belay stand, you will need sewn (webbing) slings 80 cm long. Used with a locking carabiner, these are called self-securing slings or personal anchor slings. Alternatively, an adjustable anchor sling with a central loop can be used. Two additional slings (60 and 120 cm) should be included in your kit. These can be useful for securing yourself on the ground or for the extension of slings at intermediate anchor points. Also

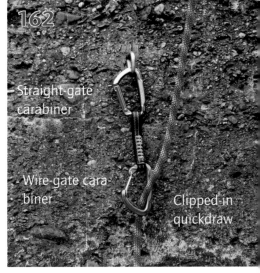

162
Straight-gate carabiner

Wire-gate cara-biner

Clipped-in quickdraw

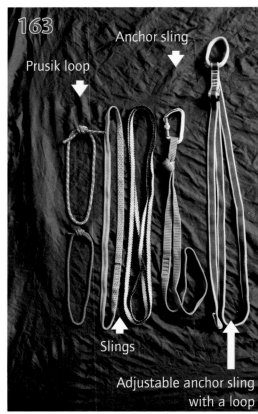

163
Anchor sling

Prusik loop

Slings

Adjustable anchor sling with a loop

two Prusik loops are required as additional protection when rappelling and when cleaning a route (Photo 163).

Information on the Climbing Area

For any popular crag or climbing area you should be able to find up-to-date information in climbing guides, or "topos." Local climbing guidebooks are available in bookshops, in on-site tourist offices, or at local climbing stores. Websites from climbing clubs in the region often include valuable information as well. Since the first steps on the rocks should always be under the watchful eye of an experienced guide, a beginner can initially rely on the knowledge of the course leader.

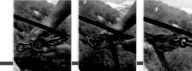
3.2 Tying Into the Climbing Harness

To tie the rope to the climbing harness, we recommend that you use the Figure Eight knot, just as in the gym. It is the most useful roping-up knot, quick to learn and, because it is easy to see, easy to check when doing buddy checks. When roping up, the rope should be threaded through both the leg loop and the waist loop (Photos 165-168).

The knot can be fixed close into the harness, which is advantageous when doing a tactical maneuver and when setting up belay stands. The rope end beyond the knot should be about a hands-length, or to be more precise, the diameter of the rope in centimeters. A rope end that is too long can get in the way when clipping in.

Waist-strap loop

Leg strap

Those who were afraid of falling when top roping in the climbing gym may want to attempt first steps in outdoor lead climbing wearing a chest and seat harness combination (see Pages 94-95). This is especially recommended where there is a danger of a head-over-heels fall. Because of the different head to body proportion, lead climbing children under 10 should always be tied in a chest and seat harness combination. Moreover, a heavy backpack generally requires a chest harness as well. Before tying into the rope, both harnesses must be connected with a sling fastened with one-sided overhand knots (breaking strain at least 22 kN with three-color strength markings) (see Page 95 Photo 158).

The length of the sling strap is dependent on the size of your body. Stretched out, the sling should be about 80-90% of your height.

The sling strap is threaded first through the central loop on the sit harness. Next a simple one-sided overhand knot is tied into the strap just above the belly button. It is important that the both strands of the webbing lay exactly on top of each other and the knot is not twisted, since twists can reduce the breaking strain of the sling. Then one end of the strap is threaded through the left loop on the chest harness, and the other end through the right loop.

Both ends are now pulled firmly together and connected with a one-sided overhand knot. It is easier to tie this knot in a slightly forward-leaning position. The sling strap is optimally attached when it hugs the body as you straighten up. The rope is now threaded through both loops of the sling, and tied with a Figure Eight knot (Photos 175 and 176).

In England and the USA, a different way of tying into chest and seat harness is popular (see Photo 177), but this method has never caught on in Europe.

TIP: *It is not necessary that the belayer is already tied into the rope when protecting the lead climber. This way, he can ensure that there are no knots or twists along the rope before he follows. Obviously, in this case the lead climber cannot check that his partner is tied in correctly. For single top-rope pitches the belayer is generally not tied in, but it is essential to tie a knot at the end of the rope, or tie it to the rope bag, so that the end of the rope cannot accidentially run through the belay device.*

3.3   Partner Safety

Belaying a partner on the lead climb requires more knowledge, attention, and practice than on a top rope.

The following points are important:

- Constantly pay attention to the actions of the lead climber.

- Alert the lead climber immediately of any mistake.

- Feed the rope quickly and carefully to permit a fluid clipping into to protection points.

- Allow as little slack as possible between the belay device and the first protection point.

- Be constantly prepared to catch a possible leader fall.

- Don't be distracted by the environment.

Just like in the gym, the belay device is usually attached to the harness of the belayer. Suitable anchor points are often difficult to find at the foot of a climb, or they are at an uncomfortable height. If the lead climber is substantially heavier than the belayer (more than 20%), the belayer should be secured to an anchor point. This could be boulders, roots, or trees (see Photos 178 and 179).

Sling secured with a fisherman's knot

Sling secured with a girth hitch knot

A sling is fixed to the anchor point (Photo 181), tied into seat harness either through the belay loop or sewn-on loops at the rear of the harness (Photos 182 and 183). In any case, the belayer must be prepared to be pulled up toward the first protection point if the leader falls. Therefore, he should also be secured by an additional anchor if the belay spot is steep, slippery, and full of loose rocks

Anchor point protection using a roping-up loop

Anchor point protection using a runner sling

Choosing Protection Equipment

Generally, you should use the same equipment for protection in lead cimbing that you used in the gym for top roping. HMS carabiners and tubers are both appropriate, and both have advantages and disadvantages. On the other hand, protection for a follow-on climber has different requirements (see Page 157).

Preparing the Rope

After putting on the harnesses, the rope is laid out and prepared. This should be easy if a rope sack was used after the preceding climb, and the end of the rope was tied into the designated loop (Photo 184). However, if the rope is severely tangled up, it must be completely unraveled, passing it through the hand from one end to the other until all knots and twists are removed. This should be done before tying in, as it is practically impossible to safely remove any knots while belaying the lead climber. For a borrowed rope unraveleling is particular

important, as one should also look for any damage. Once the rope is ready the lead climber ties himself into the top end of the rope using a Figure Eight knot (see Page 117).

For every climb, you must be certain that the rope is at least double the length of the route. Nevertheless, the free end of the rope should still be tied to the rope bag so that the belayer will be alerted just in case that the rope turns out to be too short for lowering the climber to the ground (see Page 143). Now you can feed the rope in the belay device, perform the buddy check, and the climber can start.

3.3.1 Using HMS for Belaying in Lead Climbing

Using HMS as belay is just like in top-roping—but with the distinct difference that the rope is not pulled in but fed out, giving out only as much rope as the lead climber needs. On the one hand, you don't want the rope to be too tight, as this may hinder or even endanger the lead climber ("pulling him off the wall"). On the other hand, you should prevent that too much slack prolongs a fall of the lead climber.

The optimal position of the belay stand is the same as in top-roping; it should be as close to the rock face as possible and straight below the first protection point. One should make sure that neither the rope nor the anchor point to which the belayer is tight to are crossing the fall line of the climber. It is essential to discuss the entire climb and the commands before the lead climber starts: Lowering down or rappelling after the climb? What if the climber can't reach the top? Will the belayer follow or not?

At the beginning of the climb, the belaying partner gives out enough rope so that the lead can reach the first bolt. This allows the belayer to "spot" the lead climber, that is, he positions himself behind and underneath the climber so that the belayer is able to prevent injury in case of a fall, without undue risk of injuring himself (Photo 185).

As soon as the lead climber has clipped into the first bolt, any loose rope is pulled in quickly, and and fed out again as the climb progresses. As soon as the lead climber reaches the next bolt and grabs a quickdraw from his belt, the belayer readies himself to feed out rope while still keeping the brake hand on the brake rope. Once the quickdraw is clipped into the bolt, he feeds out the rope quickly. This can be sped up by taking a step up in the direction of the first bolt. Once the rope is clipped into the lower carabiner of the quickdraw, the belayer pulls in any extra rope until he feels tension.

This tension is not problem for the lead climber—quite the opposite: For the next step he is in a quasi top-rope situation. As soon as he passes the bolt again, the rope needs to be fed out again.

Spotting for the lead climber

When the lead climber reaches the top, he clips into the anchor device (see Page 154) and calls out the command "Tension!" The belayer takes in the rope until he feels a tug on the lead rope and replies "Tension on!" As in top-roping, the climber clips onto the rope and calls out "Ready to lower!" After responding "Lowering", the belayer feeds rope into the belaying device and lets the climber down in a slow and controlled manner. More attention is needed than in the gym, as natural rock formations, particularly on easy routes, are more structured, and thus possibly require adjustments in the lowering speed.

Besides watching the climber, the belayer also checks the rope frequently, in order to spot - and loosen with the free hand - possible knots and tangles, and to be aware of the end of the rope (see Page 138).

This explanation emphasizes that belaying in lead climbing has to be practiced over and over, and in any case learned in a relaxed atmosphere. Should participation in an outdoor rock-climbing course not be possible, we recommend taking at least such a course course in the gym. However we don't believe that this alone is sufficient—as mentioned at the beginning. If you cannot do either of these, climbers inexperienced in lead climbing should initially climb together with an inexperienced rock climber. They can pick an easy route, and the experienced climber will guide the inexperienced for both, leading and following.

TIP: *If a new, extra thin rope is being used, it must be understood that it runs differently to the often very thick, roughed-up rope used in the gym. Just as smoothly as a thin rope runs through the belaying device, it will also act in case of a fall. Irrespective of whether you use a HMS or a tuber, the belaying device reacts differently for a thing rope. It can get a bit dangerous when the diameter of the rope is less than 9.8 mm. Single ropes with a diameter of less than 9.5 mm should be left to the absolute specialist.*

3.3.2 Using a Tuber Belay Device in Lead Climbing

The same principles used in top-roping in the gym are also applied here: Whenever possible, the brake hand must be positioned below the belay device. To give out rope, the brake hand feeds the rope through the tuber while the guiding hand pulls it up out of the device. Then the brake hand slips further down and feeds more rope in toward the tuber, and so on. This allows the belayer to work quickly when the lead climber needs more rope to clip in. To take in rope, the brake hand is briefly moved up above the belay device, to take in the rope, and then immediately brought back down to the lower position. If the belayer is experienced with the belay device, he can use a system where his hand slips along toward the tuber, almost completely closing over the rope. We call this "tunneling." Grabbing down onto the brake rope with the leading hand, as recommended for beginners in the gym, is omitted, resulting in a more comfortable handling method.

3.4.   What to Do in Falls

As described above, the belayer should stand as closely as possible to the rock face and near to the fall line from the first protection point. It is well possible that during a leader fall the belayer is catapulted up a little in the direction of the first protection point. The belay stand therefore has to be selected with this in mind, and the belayer must always be ready to react to any possible fall. Thus, a less experienced should always look for a flat, open area at the base of the climb. There should be no impediments such as branches or rock outcrops lying between him and the first protection point; this reduces the injury risk for the belayer.

If the belayer is pulled up by the force of the fall, he should move actively with the pull, by taking one or two steps up the rock face. One should never try to resist this impulse. The fall of the lead climber will be softened by the belayer's upward movement. Should the belayer be considerably heavier than the lead climber, he will have to consciously take these steps up toward the first protection point. This all requires a lot of practice and perfect timing. Alternatively, feeding a little rope into the HMS or tuber belaying device will help. Falling and holding falls can also be easily practiced while top-roping in the gym.

4 Lead Climbing

The first lead climb should be done in well-known terrain, on an easy climbing route with an experienced lead climber, or, even better, as part of a special lead-climbing course. In any case, the route chosen must be well within your personal limits so that you can concentrate on the new movements that you will be carrying out.

186

The lead climber must know all the points about the chosen route:

- How long is the route?
- Is the climbing rope long enough?
- How many protection points are on the route?
- What is the arrangement
  of the anchor fixture at the top?

The rope must be at least twice as long as the vertical rock face. If the route is diagonal, you will need considerably more rope. The lead climber should take at least one quickdraw more than the number of protection points in the route. The anchor arrangement on the first climb should be constructed so that once the top is reached the rope can be clipped directly into a fixed carabiner (Photo 187 or a pigtail hook (Photo 189), without the need to untie and thread the rope though a ring. If the lead climber doesn't know the route, he can find all the information needed in a topo on that area (see Page 101). Suitable areas for beginners are often indicated in these topos.

On shorter routes, the number of protection points can usually be detected from the ground.

Before the lead climber sets off, he has to discuss with his belayer whether he wants to be lowered or whether he will establish a belay stand on top and rappel down. As mentioned earlier, we recommend lowering for the first lead climbs, so that the beginner can concentrate fully on the movements used during the climb. Once the climber has gained some experience and internalized the movements, building of anchor stands and rappelling should be added (see Page 140 ff. and 158 ff.). After the route has been chosen, the lead climber can begin the preparations. A short warm-up program to loosen the muscles is always useful.

Anchor and carabiner arrangement

Pigtail

TIP: *Even when you have gained experience lead climbing, you should always start afresh after a longer winter break or when in a new climbing area and choose a route that is about two grades below your personal level. Each climbing area has its particular oddities, and details of the grade of difficulty take on a rather "local" complexion (i.e., having climbed in the Lake Garda area easily on a 5c route is not the same as a climb in the Verdon Gorge where a 5b will force you to your limits). Similarly, unusual rock surfaces and longer distances between bolts can also present etraordinary challenges.*

After putting on your harness and your helmet, you start organizing your equipment. All the required quickdraws (including one reserve) are clipped into the gear loops provided at the left and right side of the harness. The carabiner of the quickdraws that will later be clipped into the bolts is attached to the to the loops, while the other carabiner on the smaller eyelet of the quickdraw is for the rope. The reason for the differently sized eyelet loops on the quickdraw sling is as follows: The larger eyelet loop prevents the carabiner unclipping itself from the hook due to movement of the rope, while the smaller eyelet loop and the spring-loaded carabiner facilitates clipping into the rope.

The self-securing slings, the rappelling device (tuber or Figure Eight) with an HMS or locking carabiner, one to two Prusik loops, and one or two extra locking carabiners are hung onto the rear gear loops of the harness (Photos 190 and 191).

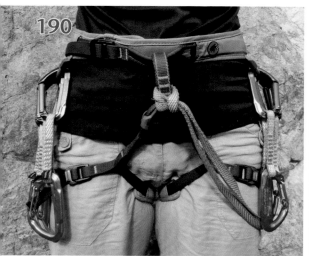

After checking the whole length of rope at least once, the lead climber ties into the rope with a Figure Eight knot positioned as close to his harness as possible (see Page 102). Wait to put on the climbing shoes until you are ready to climb so that the soles are not unnecessarily dirtied by moving around. With clay and sand on the soles, climbing shoes do not grip as well on the rocks. The belayer places the rope in the belay device. Now you do the buddy check just as before top-roping. Initially, the belayer spots the lead climber, until the climber has clipped into the first bolt (see Page 110/111).

4.1 Clipping in to the Intermediate Protection

The term "clipping in" usually means attaching the quickdraw to the protection point as well as placing the rope into the carabiner on the quickdraw. Rapid and smooth clipping in requires regular and frequent practice. Several points should be noted. First, the position of the quickdraw depends on the continuation of the route to the next bolt.

If the route leads to the left, the carabiner on the quickdraw is clipped in such a way that the gates are pointing toward the right. The locking gates must point to the left if the route leads upward to the right.

The principle is that the gates must always be pointing in the opposite direction to the climbing route (Photo 192). This prevents that the carabiner is accidentially opened and unclipped when the rope pulls the quickdraw to the side.

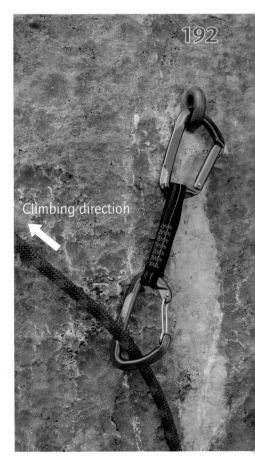

CAUTION: *Almost all manufacturers deliver quickdraws where the gate of one carabiner is pointing to the right and the other to the left. In this layout, the unit "carabiner–sling–carabiner" has the greatest strength. However, in lead climbing this layout has a distinct disadvantage: There is the constant danger that one of the gates will lay directly against the rock. When both gates point to the same side, the disadvantage of a slightly lower strength is compensated by the distinct advantage that, if the rope is used correctly, the gates are always point away from the rock (Photo 192)!*

The rope is now clipped into the lower carabiner of the quickdraw, a move that requires quite a lot of practice and also some skills, as clipping in must be mastered always with one hand only, as well as with either the right or the left hand. There are different variations. Both possibilities covered here are the most effective and also the most popular. You should practice extensively in a relaxed atmosphere at the foot of the rock or in the gym, using first your dominant hand, and then later also the non-dominant hand.

Whether you use the left or the right hand to clip in depends on your climbing position: If you have a good hold for your right hand you use the left hand to clip in and vice versa. As a rule, you must always find a stable and safe body position before you free a hand for clipping in.

a) Clipping in with the right hand with the gate on the right-hand side

The right hand grabs the rope just below the roping-up knot; the palm of the hand is facing the rock face. The rope runs over the forefinger and is held in place with the ring finger and the little finger. Thumb and middle finger hold the carabiner just below the wire gate, and the forefinger pushes the rope into the carabiner (Photos 193-194). This should be done in a quick, flowing motion; otherwise there is a danger that the forefinger will become pinched in the wire gate as it closes. This method ensures that the rope is running correctly through the carabiner (i.e., from below, along the rock face through the carabiner up to the lead climber) (Photo 196).

Photos 193-196: Clipping in with the right hand with the wire gate on the right hand side

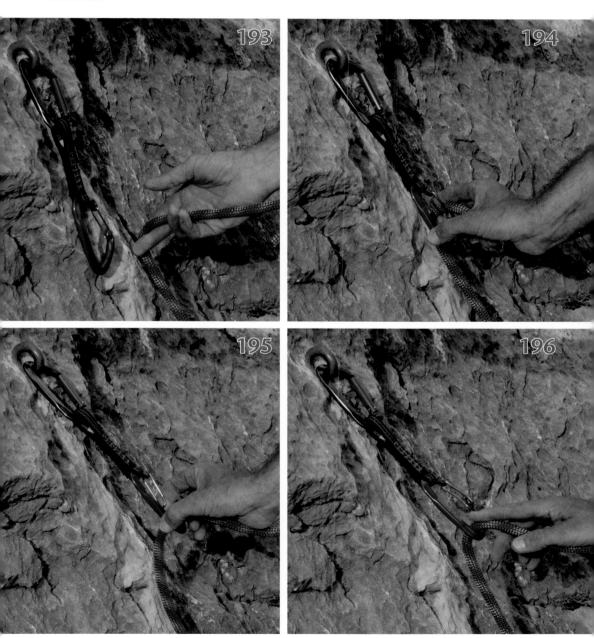

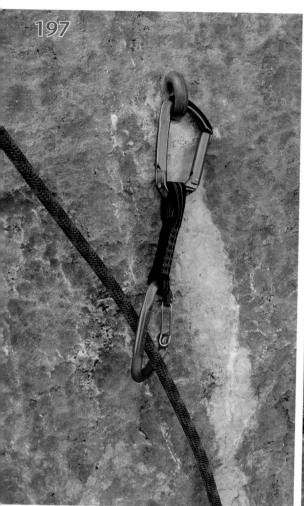

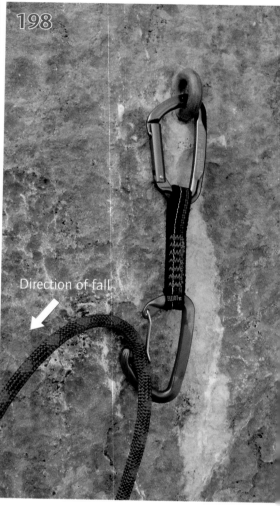

Direction of fall

CAUTION: *If the rope is clipped in the other way round (i.e., the rope comes up from below over and into the carabiner and then up along the rock face to the lead climber), the carabiner will twist as the climb progresses (Photo 197). Contact with the rock could then open the carabiner gate slightly, which would reduce the breaking strength of the carabiner considerably. Should the wire gate position also be incorrect, the rope could become unclipped in case of a fall.*

One has to consciously work against the deceptive feeling that early clipping in means safety. The following points will help:

- When one clips into the first bolt is really not important. The second climber is spotting until the rope is in the carabiner and then takes over the responsibility for belaying. Before the first bolt is reached, a fall will always end on the ground or in the arms of the second climber.
- The second protection point should be clipped in at the level of the roping-in knot (Photos 213 and 214).
- The third bolt should be at shoulder height (Photo 215), and
- The fourth bolt should be at eye level when clipping in.

As a rule, clipping in is always done from a stable position where one hand can be safely released from the rock face.

CAUTION: *Even on upper parts of a route, don't clip in to a protection point where you have to stretch up to do so. If you do, your handholds and footholds will be less stable. Remember, just before clipping you are at the maximum height for a potential fall!*

On more difficult climbing routes or climbs with overhangs, it is possible that the crux requires freeing one hand from the rock for clipping in to a protection point. In those cases, sometimes the protection points are pre-prepared with quickdraws, so that clipping in can be done as quickly as possible. Beginning lead-climbers should not get too used to this, because this is not always possible without problems, and moreover, correct clipping helps building the mental strength required for leading. Those who have done lead climbing in the gym are likely familiar with pre-prepared quickdraw slings, as gym climbing routes are often laid out in this manner.

Yet, one must be careful: The placement of the quickdraws is not always optimal for the continuing climb, as a bolt can serve several different routes. Climbers used to climbing in such gyms must concentrate on the correct placement of their quickdraws; even experienced climbers often make mistakes in this regard.

TIP: *If the lead climber finds that he is carrying too few quickdraws, the belayer will have to lower him down a few meters from the bolt so that he can unclip the necessary quickdraws and gather them up. However, only the third to last quickdraw can be unclipped. Later ones have to remain clipped in for redundancy. Should even more quickdraws be required, it is better to lower the climber to the ground, and collect sufficient equipment at the base.*

4.2   Ropeline

For the optimal ropeline one has to consider the way the rope runs along the body of the lead climber, as well as the way the rope runs in the entire climbing route. In a fall, the correct ropeline along the body is paramount for avoiding injuries. If the lead climber is standing in the fall line above the last protection point, the rope has to run down centrally between his legs (Photo 216).

If the climber is offset above the protection point, the rope runs over the foot or the thigh of the leg closest to the bolt (Photo 217-220).

Sometimes even practiced climbers neglect to correctly guide the rope, because they concentrate too much on the difficulty of the climb. Unfortunately, this happens most often when climbing at their limit, where the danger of a fall is at its greatest.

Girth hitch

Both the lead climber and the belayer should always keep a sharp eye on the correct path of the rope. In a fall, incorrect guidance can lead to a backward somersault and a heavy hit on the head and back.

The lead climber must note how the rope runs along the route so that there is not too much friction as it passes through the protection. If the rope runs poorly, it becomes more difficult to pull the rope up when clipping in, up to the point that continuing climbing may become impossible.

There can be lots of friction where the bolts are far apart horizontally, or when climbing over small roofs and overhangs. In those cases, one must extra-long quickdraws to clip in the respective bolts, in order to straighten the path of the rope.

If these are not available, a sewn web can be threaded through the bolt via a girth hitch (Photo 221), which in turn is connected to the rope with a single carabiner or a quickdraw sling (Photo 222).

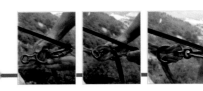

4.3   At the Anchor Point

Once the lead climber has reached the top, he clips the rope into the anchor provided. In many cases, the arrangement consists of two cemented bolts connected with a chain. In one of the bolts you will find either

a) a special top-rope carabiner (Photo 223),
b) a pigtail hook (Photo 224),
c) a wrought iron chain (Photo 225), or
d) a large locking chain link (Photo 226).

With the arrangements in a) and b) above, the lead climber merely needs to place his rope in the anchor. If it is fitted with a chain or a chain link as in c) and d), the lead climber has to rearrange (see Page 132 ff.). This action should not be undertaken on the first lead climb, but after gaining some experience with this arrangement. Those who have top-roped will know what follows: The climber calls out "Up rope!" and waits for the response from the belayer—"O.K. On belay!"—who checks that the rope is taut. The climber then calls clearly, "Ready to lower!" As he is lowered, the climber collects in all the quickdraws. First, he unclips the rope from the quickdraw and then takes the quickdraw off the bolt (Photos 227-230). He does this using both hands so that he doesn't accidentially drop a quickdraw. The recommended sequence for rappelling— unclip the quickdraw at the anchor bolt, hang it onto your climbing harness, and only then free the rope—awkward for lowering down and particularly exhausting on steep ground.

CAUTION: *If leaving the rope in the anchor for further top-roping, the last quickdraw before the anchor must also be left clipped in for redundancy. While it is extremely unlikely that an anchor point will break off, it is theoretically possible if bolts are incorrectly placed or the quality of the rock is poor.*

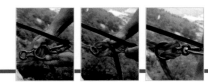
4.4 Repositioning, Threading the Rope, and Lowering

To thread the rope—in the process of repositioning—there are two variations. In both, the climber first fixes himself with his self-securing sling on the anchor point (Photo 231). One should make sure that this sling does not get in the way when threading the rope. If there are two fixed bolts or a double ring, the upper-anchor fixing should be used to attach the sling. It will now be obvious why the locking carabiner on the self-securing sling has such a small shank diameter, as it should fit in any chain link or bolt even when a chain link or carabiner is already attached to it. After locking the carabiner, the climber leans back into the self-securing sling and calls out "Slack!" The belayer feeds out about 3-4 m of rope without taking the climber off belay. Now threading the rope begins.

231

The climber now loosens the one-sided overhand bend (Photo 242) and calls out "Off belay!" He puts weight on his personal anchor sling and waits for the response from his partner, "On belay!", and on the tightening of the rope to know that he is again hanging in to the belayer's protection point. After a final check to see if everything is threaded properly and that he is tied in correctly, he unclips from the anchor point and calls out "down!" (Photos 243 and 244)

b) The quicker version is the blunt-threading method of threading (Photos 245-252). The climber secures himself and pulls in enough rope. He threads the rope with a loop through the ring. He now ties a one-sided overhand bend with a large loop and attaches this to the locking carabiner on the tie-in loop on his harness, locking the gate right away. The climber then unties the rope and calls to the belayer below, "Off belay!" The procedure from here is the same as described in a) above.

CAUTION: *During the lowering, the belayer must carefully observe the climber so that he can stop giving out rope as the climber gathers the quickdraws. In addition, the belayer must constantly watch the remainder of the rope so that no twists or knots block the belaying device. Similarly, he watches the end of the rope so that it doesn't run out before the climber has reached the ground safely. What happens next is described on Page 62.*

5   Rappelling

In contrast to gym climbing, rappelling is a basic part of the skills to be learned for outdoor rock climbing, since it is often the only possibility to gain solid ground back under the feet again!

As a rule, the mechanics of repositioning at anchor points and rappelling should be learned on the ground under supervision, and only then applied to a complete climb on an easy route.

253

5.1 Preparation and Repositioning at Anchor Points

If you are going to rappel, the lead climber must carry the following equipment on his harness (Photo 254):

- **A rappelling device:** A Figure Eight plus a locking carabiner or tuber plus HMS. Do not use a slim locking carabiner with the tuber, because when rappelling, the bend of the tuber tends to trap the rope. To avoid this, the rope and the tuber must be attached to the broader side of the HMS carabiner (i.e., quite the opposite to using the tuber on protection points) (see Page 145). The Figure Eight is carried with the larger eyelet in the locking carabiner on the harness.
- **A self-securing sling with a locking carabiner:** This should be as small as possible and have a small shank diameter so that it can be used on very small protection point bolts or in an emergency connected to a link chain. This is particularly important when cleaning an uncompleted route (see Page 166 ff.), because in these cases the locking carabiner has to be fitted together with a quickdraw or a rope onto the hook (Photo 255). The HMS carabiner is too thick for this.
- **A Prusik loop 5 or 6 mm together with a locking carabiner.** Having a second Prusik loop of a different diameter loop as reserve is also useful.

At the top, first the personal protection sling is attached onto a secure anchor point. If two bolts are available, the upper one should be used (Photo 256). In this way there is sufficient room below the belay point to thread the rope and reposition yourself (cf., Chapter 4.3, Page 132 ff.).

If the anchor point consists of just one bolt with a single ring, the self-securing sling and the rope are both attached to this (Photo 257). If the bolt has two rings or a separate chain link, the self-securing sling is attached to the upper ring (Photo 258) or directly in the bolt (Photo 259). The ring or chain link is used later for the rope.

You now put weight on the personal protection sling. To do this, lean or step back until the sling is tense and then call out the command, "Off belay!" The belayer removes the protection for the lead climber and calls back, "Belay off!" He then remains at his stand and watches the lead climber and his further actions. The lead climber now gathers some rope and feeds a loop of it through a free chain link or the free ring. He threads the rope through the anchor pulley until he reaches the middle marking on the rope or his belayer calls out, "Rope out!" This is when the lower end of the rope is still just on the ground.

CAUTION: *When the command "Rope out!" is heard and the middle marking on the rope is still well below the anchor pulley, the rope is too short for rappelling. The climber must therefore come part way down and construct a rappel anchor, and rappel from there to the ground.*

The lead climber now unties from the rope and pulls the remainder of the rope through the chain link or ring. He then ties a knot in the end of the rope, and after calling out "Rope!" he throws the rope parallel to the other strand in the direction of the start of the climb. Especially in easy routes that are not very steep the rope will not land directly on the ground, but often gets caught up somewhere on the rocks. (It is not necessary to pull up the rope and try again, as the rope will normally come free when rappelling. One should just watch out for loops and knots and untangle them before rappelling further.) Now, the climber prepares the rappeling device. He starts with the short Prusik sling.

5.2   Using the Prusik Knot when Rappelling

The Prusik knot is named after its inventor Dr. Karl Prusik, an Austrian climber and member of the Austrian Alpine Club, who opened up Alpine climbing routes during the first half of the 20th Century and has many first ascents to his credit. For back-up protection when rappelling, a short Prusik sling can be used—this is different to the Prusik loop that is used for self-rescue after falling in a crevasse.

The exact length of the Prusik sling depends, among other things, on the size of your body. It must be long enough that it can be moved easily during rappelling, but not so long that it could get caught in the rappelling device—it would not be possible to free it while hanging in the rope. Therefore, everyone must determine the appropriate length of the Pruski sling for himself. The length is about right when the distance between the knot and the carabiner is roughly four fingers (Photo 266). Its diameter depends on the thickness of the climbing rope: For thinner ropes, i.e. with a diameter of less than 10 mm, the cord should be 5 mm—while thicker ropes require 6 mm. Thin Prusik slings will lock faster, while thicker ones mover more easily along the rope.

The Prusik sling is a really brilliant piece of safety equipment when rappelling. Depending on the diameter of the climbing rope, the ends of the approximately 89-90 cm long cord—5-6 mm thick—are tied together using a double fisherman's knot (Photos 260-265).

After the knot is tied, the length of the ends of the cord in cm should equal the thickness of the cord in mm (e.g., cord=5 mm/end length 5 cm).

TIP: *As Prusik slings are inexpensive, it should not be a problem to carry several with different diameters and lengths with you on your harness.*

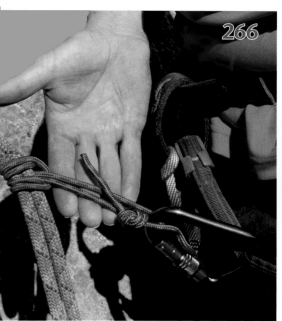

Rock Climbing

a) Rappelling using a tuber

Now the finished Prusik sling is looped twice around the double strand of the rope, forming the Prusik knot. The knot should be located just below the rappelling device and pulled lightly together. It is then attached with a locking carabiner to the brake-hand side leg strap contact with the carabiner will reduce the breaking strength of the cord. Then the pull on the rope between anchor point and Prusik knot is reduced. This makes it easier to prepare the

rappelling device. As you rappel, the Prusik knot is moved along the rope with the brake hand (Photo 276 and 282). Now the two strands of the rope are placed from above into the two slits of the tuber parallel to the hook element. The climber clips both ropes and the hook element into the broader side of the HMS carabiner and locks it up (Photos 273 -275).

b) Rappelling using a Figure Eight

The short Prusik sling is attached to the double strand of the rope and the pull on the rope is reduced. Figure Eight is attached to the tie-in loop on the harness using a locking carabiner. The carabiner is placed in the larger eye of the Figure Eight (Photo 277). The climber then threads a loop of double stand of the rope through the larger eye and places the loop over the smaller eye. This way the Figure Eight cannot slip out when doing the changeover to the smaller eye (Photos 277-281). As you rappel, the Prusik knot is moved along the rope with the brake hand (Photo 276 and 282).

Photos 277-282 show the handling of the Prusik for left-handed climbers. If the brake hand is the right hand, the locking carabiner for the Prusik cord is attached to the right-hand leg strap on the harness.

279

280

281

arabiner attached
the leg strap

282

283

286

287

The Prusik functions through a clamping effect. If you take your hand off the Prusik, the knot will tighten, and you are now hanging by the climbing rope (i.e., you cannot rappel more) (Photos 283-289). Taking the weight of the rope briefly will loosen the sling, and you can continue rappelling. These actions and clamping the Prusik should be practiced on the ground.

If the sling locks onto the climbing rope (e.g., on overhanging ground), it is not easy to free it without a lot of struggling. There are two ways out of this situation:

1. The partner on the ground pulls hard on the rope in order to lighten the load on the sling which then can be released.
2. The rapelling climber wraps the rope 2-3 times around his foot while bending his knee. Once he straightens his leg, the load on the knot will be lightened, and the Prusik will come free (Photos 290-293).

These actions are best practiced in a relaxed atmosphere on an overhanging wall in the gym.

CAUTION: *While the clamping effect of the Prusik should be tested under appropriate supervision, it should be avoided in rappelling. The ways out described above are very difficult to use if you are under stress.*

5.3 Rappelling and Removing the Intermediary Protection

After attaching the Prusik loop, the climber loosens his self-securing strap by pulling himself up towards the anchor using the rappelling device (Photos 294 and 295). This requires some practice and good timing particularly on steep and slippery stands. When he loosens the self-securing strap, he keeps the brake hand on the Prusik loop and the rappel begins. The brake hand remains close to the thigh on the knot of the Prusik loop and pushes it along during the rappel. This ensures fluid rappelling.

At each intermediary protection point, the climber stops and removes it as follows: First the carabiner is unclipped from the bolt and clipped onto the gear loop of the harness. Subsequently, the climbing rope is unclipped from the other carabiner. This action must be carried out with the guiding hand alone. The brake hand remains on the Prusik loop and keeps this this loose (Photos 296-299).

You must remove any twists and unravel the rope with the one hand as you rappel. If the rope has to be thrown down again the command "Rope!" must be repeated. Once the climber reaches the base, he removes the Prusik and the rappelling device off the rope and pulls the rope down. Just before the rope end passes through the anchor, he warns other climbing parties about the falling rope by giving the call "Rope!"

294

295

Direction of pull

296

297

298

299

TIP: *Tuber and Figure Eight rappelling devices can become very hot on long rappelling distances. One can avoid touching the device and pontial burns by keeping the rope loose.*

After a lead climb, rappelling is generally preferable to lowering down. It is easier to unclip the carabiners at the bolts because the rope is not under strain. Moreover, rappelling is much more gentle on the rope than lowering. Time is at the essence when the weather changes suddenly, especially in multi-pitch routes, and therefore rappelling should be practiced as often as possible. This will make repositioning and threading safer, and the procedure will become automatic and quick.

300

301

Even though advanced climbers and climbing instructors may rappell without Prusik sling, we strongly recommend to always use it. There is no better and cheaper life insurance!

TIP: *On overhanging terrain, unclipping quickdraws while rappelling can be very tiring. In such cases it may be better to lower the lead climber so that he has both hands free for cleaning the route. By connecting the other strand of the rope to the harness with a quickdraw one can prevent swinging away from the rock (Photos 300-303). Even then, a little pull toward the rock face is required to facilitate unclipping. This is somewhat exhausting and requires practice.*

302

303

Rock Climbing

6 Belaying and Rappelling in a Team

In preparation for multi-pitch routes, you should practice belaying the second climber from the top and then rappelling down together. Before doing this in an outdoor climb, you should practice under supervision of an experienced lead climber to set up the belay stand and the technique of belaying from above.

6.1 Setting Up a Belay Stand and Belaying

The lead climb has carried out as described in chapter 4. Once reaching the anchor point, the climber secures himself first using the self-securing strap (see Page 132).

As he sets up the belay stand, the lead climber should plan ahead and consider the best position for his partner once completing the pitch, to his right or to his left. His self-securing strap is positioned with this in mind (Photo 304).

304

Second climber

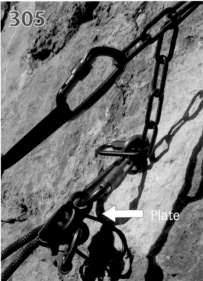
305

Plate

306

When he has closed the locking carabiner and putting weight on the self-securing sling, the climber calls out "Off belay!" The belayer unclips the rope from the belay device and calls back "Belay off!" The lead climber now pulls in the rope while the belayer keeps his eye on the the rope still lying on the ground so it does not twist or get tangled at the first protection point. Before the end of the rope is reached, he calls out "Rope end!" The lead climber now balays the second climber from the anchor. He places the belay device onto the bolt below his own self-securing strap (Photo 304) so that he can handle the rope when belaying the second climber. Photos 304-307 show different belay set-ups with HMS and Sticht plate, Photo 311 the classic set-up with the climbing rope, and Photo 156 the use of an adjustable self-securing sling (see Page 176). In the meantime, the second climber has tied himself in and waits for the command "On Belay!" He answers, calling "Climbing!" and waits until the rope is pulled in tight. He now climbs up and gathers all the protection placed on the climb.

CAUTION: *Only HMS or Sticht plate (e.g., ATC-guide, Reverso [see Page 96 ff.]) are suitable for belaying in this case. Standard tubers or Figure Eights cannot be used for the belay from top! Because the lead strand and the braking strand of the rope run parallel when belaying a following climber, the braking power of these devices is not strong enough to catch a fall.*

Belaying a following climber also requires considerable practice and clear commands: the rope cannot be too tight, so that the protection can be unclipped without a problem, but too much slack is risky and stresses the nerves of the following climber. If both climbers are in sight of each other, the right tension will normally not be a problem. However, if the belayer cannot see the following climber, he may hear the command "Up rope!" more frequently. If, on the other hand, the climber needs more slack so that he can unclip protection, he calls out "Slack!" The belayer then feeds out just 50 cm of rope and takes in back in when hearing the command "Up rope!".

6.2   At the Belay Stand

Having arrived at the preplanned belay stand, the second climber immediately secures himself with his self-securing strap. The lead climber has already decided which side his partner will be positioned—left or right. The choice relies on the terrain and the set-up of the belay stand. For first-time climbers, a well-known, easy route with plenty of room for the belay stand is recommended.

After the second climber has secured himself, the lead climber takes him off the belay, then unties and threads the rope through the rappel anchor. Unlike the procedure seen on page 144, the early unclipping here is not a problem. Because the second climber is still tied in the rope, it cannot fall down by accident. Once the center of the rope has reached the rappel anchor, the second climber also unties from the rope. The ends are tied together and, after calling "Rope!", the rope it is thrown down towards the start of the pitch.

6.3   Rappelling

First, the less experienced climber prepares himself for rappelling and starts to rappel down. When he reaches the base of the rock face, he unclips himself and calls out "Rappel off!" Before the partner begins to rappel, he checks that the rope around the anchor is properly laid so that the rope can later be pulled off easily.

7   Falling Correctly

Falls when climbing are unavoidable. While small slips or swing-outs when top-roping close to one's ability are common, falls by a lead-climbing beginner should be the exception. It is of particular importance to be able to control a leader fall with the appropriate technique. It, therefore, makes sense to practice how to fall correctly in easier climbs before attempting to lead more difficult routes.

7.1   Practicing Falling

The ideal practice terrain is a close to vertical, or even better, overhanging rock face that can be well protected. Of course, one also needs a partner with experience in catching leader falls. The practice site should not be too close to the ground, because the less rope is fed out, the greater the impact force will be (i.e., the force that the rope effects on the body of the climber and the belayer when holding the fall), due to of lack of significant rope stretch.

Immediately before practicing a fall, it is best to warn the belayer that you are about to do so. The climber should now try to push himself away from the rock face with his hands and feet, so that he is not caught on rocky outcrops below (Photo 156). He should however not push himself away too far, as this will cause a much harder impact when swinging back to the rock face. On an overhanging route, it is sufficient to just let go of any holds. To adopt a good landing position, hips and knees should be slightly bent, the stomach muscles tensed and the torso pushed slightly forward.

Many climbers experienced in falling grab onto the rope above the tie-in knot as they fall. This helps to stabilize the position of the body and is a particularly good idea in long falls (Photo 310). However, one must avoid by all means to accidentially grap the reverse strand of the rope, as this may lead to considerable burns. The impact against the rock face is absorbed with outstretched feet and additionally cushioned by bent knees and hip joints (Photos 314 and 318). The first practice falls should be carried out close to the last intermediate protection point. If you are particularly anxious, you could let yourself fall from just below the top bolt, with a little slack. Then your first leader fall will be no more than a fall when top-roping.

For the follow-up practice falls, the length of the falls should be increased slowly as follows: Without the belayer feeding rope in or out, the climber climbs up higher, until the knees are at the level of the top bolt (Photo 315). This should be possible without feeding out rope, as the preceding practice fall pulled some rope through the belay device. From this position, the climber lets himself fall again. The next practice fall is done when the feet are at the level of the bolt.

Rock Climbing

CAUTION: *Falling, even in a practice setting, is not without risk of injury, particularly to the inexperienced climber or when the area is not optimal. Therefore, it is advisable to begin practice falls from a top-rope position. By gradually increasing the amount of slack rope, one can safely increase the fall height. As a rule: No practice falls without a helmet. There also is a certain amount of risk of injury to the belayer, especially when inattentive or positioned incorrectly.*

TIP: *Those who are already afraid of falling when top-roping certainly need to systematically learn falling correctly without fear. The first attempts are best carried out on top-rope in the gym. Each time you practice, do it unannounced. When*

climbing at the limits falls will happen regularly anyway. Soon one will try out moves once thought unattainable, and experience falls from various climbing positions. Besides losing excessive fear of falling, this training has the added advantage thar the climber no longer hesitates when attempting a difficult climb. He learns to make quick decisions, adopts a more fluid climbing style, and is generally faster. This increases the chances of completing climbs at the limit without a fall. In the gym, the climber will be able to tackle more routes than before, and will successfully complete his projects with fewer attempts. Practicing falls is also good experience for the belayer. He learns to react quickly and correctly, and trains his reflexes when catching falls (cf., Chapter 3.4, Page 115).

8 Bailing Out and Cleaning

When the lead climber cannot, or does not want to, climb on after a fall, he has to clean off the route from the highest bolt reached. This means to stop the route before reaching the top belay stand, and to start the descent from a bolt in the route. Of course, he could also be lowered down by his partner who then can attempt to complete the climb. If this is not possible, the climber fixes himself in the last bolt with the self securing sling, and gives the appropriate command. What follows depends on the type of anchor point.

If the bolt eye is large enough to accommodate the self-securing sling and the rope, one can thread the climbing rope through the bolt and subsequently be lowered down or rappel down. or. With bolts that have sharp edges, one has to rappel (Photo 322), as lowering down would damage the rope. Since the sharp bend is not optimal for rappelling, either, it would be more gentle on the rope to thread a thicker (6-7 mm) Prusik sling twice through the bolt, and rappel down through the sling (Photos 322-324).

Of course, the Prusik sling will have to remain on the route in most cases, since one is only very rarely lucky enough that the Prusik sling also comes off when the rope is pulled down. The sling must be inspected for any damage before using it again.

The variant "screw link" (Photos 325 and 326) is the preferred alternative: For such cases one needs to carry one oval screw link on the harness, which will be used in an analogous manner as the Prusik sling, for lowering down. With a screw link, one can also rappel.

CAUTION: *A Prusik sling must neverbe used for lowering down. The friction of the rope on the sling material would heat and melt the mantle; after only a few meters of rappelling the sling would break Even when threading the rope through the Prusik sling before rappelling, one hast to be careful not to damage the sling. Although the rope is not under strain, strong continuous pull could lead to heat damage on the thin mantle of the belay sling. It is better to push the rope through the sling rather than pull it (Photo 323).*

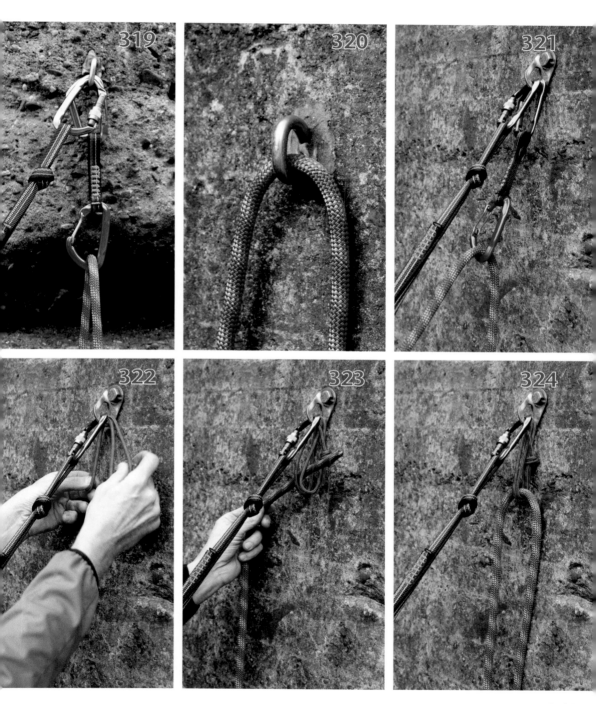

For most newer bolts, both, the carabiner on the quickdraw and the small locking carabiner of the self-securing sling fit together in to the eye (Photo 319). This may not be possible for some older bolts. In such cases, the climber has to thread a belay sling (doubled) intot the bolt and secure himself to this. There will be sufficient room to unclip the quickdraw and thread the rope through the eyelet, or to attach the screw-link.

If there is an easier route directly next to the uncompleted climbing route, one can take it as a very safe alternative. The lead climber is lowered using the last clipped-in quickdraw. The rope remains also clipped in the previous bolt, for redundancy. The remaining quickdraws are collected (cleaned off) and the rope removed. After climbing the easier adjacent route, the two remaining quickdraws can be collected while rappelling.

CAUTION: *The climbing partners have to agree before the climb whether the leader will be rappelling or lowered down – even in case of a retreat. This is particularly important on longer routes, where limited contact can lead to misunderstandings and possibly accidents. If lowering, the command "Off belay!" must never be given. If after a fall, the climber can neither rappel nor be lowered, the belayer must block the belay device before initiating other actions (see Page 190 ff.).*

TIP: *If you can feel sharp edges on the bolt eye that could have been caused by numerous falls, then you should avoid being lowered down but rappel down. It is better to use a screw-link rather than a Prusik sling (Photos 325 and 326).*

CAUTION: *If the lead climber does not have the correct equipment with him, he must never try to improvise. It is better to be lowered from the last quickdraw, grab what is required, and then top-rope up and clean off correctly.*

9 Multi-pitch Routes

Many new outdoor climbers stay with single-pitch routes that have the character of a climbing garden, even after they gained more experience on the rock. Lead climbing is exciting enough, and the joy of climbing on a perfectly laid-out route in a relaxed atmosphere is more value to them than the adventure of being left to themselves for hours on a rock face often higher than 100 m.

However, there are climbers who wish to dabble a little with the idea to climb big walls. They dream of lots of air below their feet and glance at the high peaks that are quite often near a beginner-friendly climbing garden. How you can safely realize this dream—step by step—is described in the following chapter.

We have deliberately not included Alpine climbing, because the seriousness of such routes and the numerous factors that must be taken into consideration with this variation of our climbing sport are not suitable for the outdoor beginner.

328

9.1 Tactics, Choice of Route, and Special Preparation

Just as with the first lead climb, one should pick for the first multi-pitch climb a route that is well within one's personal limits. Since one is often for several hours on a rock face, far away from the safety of the ground, these climbs are very serious undertakings. In addition, the choice of the correct partner becomes more important. The best team consists of two equally strong partners whose experience and climbing ability match well. Still, it is advantageous to tackle the first multi-pitch route with an experienced climber.

329

Rock Climbing

The route to be climbed should be well protected and not longer than 2-3 short pitches. Since you cannot see the whole route at the start of the climb— often the topos do not contain all the information for each pitch (e.g., the number of bolts and the type of belay stands)—it is better to take just a little more equipment with you than normal. A medium-sized backpack is recommended for each person.

For lead climbing, it is useful to also take the following items in addition to the usual basic equipment:

- 2 quickdraws
- 2 Prusik slings (5 and 6 mm)
- 2 webbing slings (60 and 120 cm)
- An adjustable anchor sling with a loop
- An additional HMS carabiner
- An additional locking carabiner

For routes of more than 3 or 4 pitches drinks, granola bars, light all-weather protection, a First Aid kit, and a cell phone should be included in the belayer's backpack. Such climbs often may take half a day, especially for inexperienced climbers. If the descent is not rappel but a hike down, firm shoes are also required. Descending in climbing shoes is not only very uncomfortable, but outright dangerous.

Multi-pitch routes often are located in more remote areas; in such cases, one needs to plan for the longer ascent to the beginning of the climb as well.

330

The calanques rocks near Marseille and...

TIP: *In many climbing areas there are easy one rope-length routes with several possible belay stands within the pitch. In these one can easily practice all the procedures for multi-pitch climbing. All the necessary information is normally contained in the topo for that area.*

331

...the Quiquillon above Orpierre offer ideal conditions for your first multi-pitch routes.

9.2   Leading, Building Belay Stands, and Following

All preparatory work at the base of the climb is as described in chapter 4. On shorter routes, one can leave both backpacks at the base of the climb. Leading, building belay stands, and following are also the same as already covered. Normally, the partners should alternate leading in multi-pitch climbs, and thus the lead climber must consider the next pitch and position himself accordingly when building the belay stand.

This means: if the follower comes up on the right and is going to climb up further to the right-hand side, the lead climber should position himself in the belay stand as far left as possible. If the climb continues on the left-hand side (i.e., the second climber has to cross over the belay stand), the first climber needs to decide whether it is better to step over above or below the belay stand. He then positions himself so that interference is minimized.

TIP: *If the first protection point on the second rope length is way off from the belay stand or the moves upward appear difficult, it may be advisable to clip a quickdraw into the upper bolt on the belay stand as a "**dummy runner**" (Photo 332). This reduces the potential fall distance as well as the impact of the fall on body and protection a little. It is, however, only useful when there are two bolts at the belay stand and the upper one is in the direction of the climb. Otherwise the rope from the falling lead climber could run over the hands and arms of the belayer.*

9.3 Belaying the Lead Climber from the Belay Stand

As described above, the lead climber arranges himself in the belay stand so that the second climber can continue climbing up without a problem. For a comfortable, well-functioning position it can be advantageous to clip the personal anchor sling into one of the chain links. This is useful for example when the route continues beside the higher bolt of the belay anchor. One clips the personal anchor sling into the second or third chain link, and belays the lead climber from the upper bolt (Photo 333). If one wants to belay from the lower bolt instead, which is opposite to the continuation of the route, a dummy runner should be used to allow for more fluid movement of the rope.

333

Lead climber

Personal anchor sling

Should the stand consist just of two bolts, and no chain, an adjustable anchor sling is clipped into both bolts, and both the personal protection and the belay device is clipped into the central loop (Photo 334, Semmel 2009). For better handling of the belay device it may sometimes be advantageous to clip the personal protection into the second bolt. This also assures redundancy, as the load is distributed onto two fixed points. If there is only one bolt at the belay stand, a locking carabiner is clipped in as the central protection point, and both the personal protection and the belay device is clipped into this carabiner. Similarly, if the bolt contains a large ring, this serves as the central protection point for personal protection and belay (Photo 335).

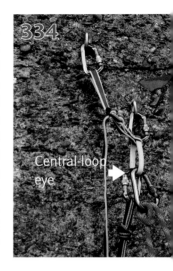

Central-loop eye

Before the second climber continues on climbing the next pitch, a buddy check is carried out and, if required, equipment is handed over. The belayer puts weight on his personal anchor sling and belays the new lead climber carefully, with as little slack rope as possible. As the climber reaches the belay stand at the end of the second pitchhe calls out the command "Off belay!" as soon as he has secured himself. His belaying partner calls back "Belay off!", takes him off the belay, but remains secured with his personal anchor sling. The lead climber pulls in the remainder of the rope, and, after his partner calls out "Rope end!", takes him on belay and ives the rope command "On Belay"

The second climber unclips his sling, calls out "Climbing!", and begins to climb as soon as he feels a tug on his rope. If there is too much slack he calls out "Up rope!" and waits until he feels a tug on the rope again. When at an overhang or a traverse the rope needs to be less tight, he calls out "Slack!". If the climber cannot feel that rope is being fed out, he has to pull it toward his body. After the climbing move he calls out again "Up rope!"

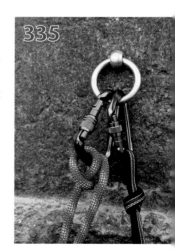

These actions may occur several times during the following climber's ascent, especially when there is belayer and climber are not in visual contact. In such cases belaying must particularly careful and sensitive, both for the leader and the following climber. Generally it is better for the lead climber to have a few centimeters more slack than to constantly feel the downward pull of the rope. The following climber, on the other hand, can be belayed a little tighter. Just for unclipping bolts, a little rope must be fed out on the command "Slack!". It is clear that for a smooth climb on multi-pitch routes, particularly in blind spots of the terrain, there has to be a lot more communication

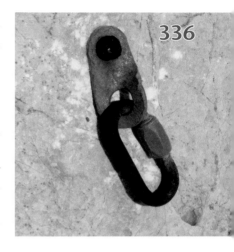

between the partners than on single-pitch climbs where there is almost always visual contact.

CAUTION: *If the belay station does not look safe (e.g., rusty or loose bolts [Photo 336], crumbling rocks, or hollow-sounding rock face in the area of the anchor points), one should abandon the climb and rappel. If even this is too risky, the climber has to return to the last, solid protection point and begin the retreat from there.*

TIP: *There is often a solid anchor point at the base of a single-pitch route where belaying a lead climber can be practiced. The anchor point, however, should be at a reasonable height (i.e., at hip or shoulder height).*

CAUTION: *Generally, we do not recommend that outdoor beginners belay from the body. In this passive belay system (where the belay device is attached to the harness rather than to a fixed point on the rock face), the body is part of the belay chain and if the leader falls, the belayer will always be pulled upward and against the rock face. The correct reaction and the catching of a fall from a body belay requires a lot of practice, and hence one should belay from fixed points at the belay stand whenever possible.*

9.4　Changing Over at the Belay Station

If only one of the partners is going to lead on a multi-pitch route, a change over at each belay station is required. This occurs as follows: The lead climber plans the route further up from the belay station and decides where his partner will stand when he arrives. After reaching the station, the follower clips his personal anchor sling into the place indicated and puts weight on it. After taking his partner off belay and taking any equipment he has collected off him, the lead climber is put on belay. After a short discussion on further action and a buddy check, the lead climber unclips his securing sling and begins to climb the next rope length.

Having one climber leading all pitches should be an exception. On longer routes, the pitches can be arranged so that the better climber can lead on the more difficult sections. In this way, the climbers alternately get some rest, and both can share the enjoyment of lead climbing.

337

9.5   Rappelling and Climbing Down

On multi-pitch routes there are often several ways of descending:

* One can rappel down the route just climbed.
* In mountainous regions there are often several pre-prepared rappelling routes. Generally, these can be reached over easy terrain from the summit.
* One can come down using an easy path or track. For this type you must have firm shoes with some profile on the sole.
* Perhaps there is a via ferrata that can be used for a quick descend. If it is demanding, a via ferrata self-belay set should be used (Photo 338).

It is essential to obtain information about the descent options before starting the climb.

On the first shorter practice runs, rappelling down the route climbed will be the norm. One must, however, consider that other parties may be on their climb up the same route. In such cases, knowledge about possible alternatives will be helpful:

* Can one rappel down an adjacent route where there are no climbers coming up?
* Is the rope long enough for the distances between belay stands on that route?
* Is the terrain suitable for rappelling?
* Can the alternative route reached safely from the end of your own route?

Preparation for rappelling and actual rappelling are described in chapter 5. However, several important points should be kept in mind. While climbing up, one should watch out for the following details:

- Construction of the belay stands
- Length of individual pitches
- Terrain and course of the route

If in bad weather, some belay stands may be difficult to find when rappelling. Extra care is required on traversing routes. Once swung out of the route, it is often only possible to reach the next belay station through strenuous and risky pendulum moves. In this case, it is helpful to clip in one or two quickdraws when rappelling, for the benefit of the following climber and to reduce the own backward pull when traversing. At the next belay station the rope should be loose, with slack, so that the partner does not swing back when unclipping the slings. Feeding out some slack is important, as it is impossible to rappel on a tighly fixed rope. Closer to the belay stand the first climber can pull the partner towards himself.

it is generally advisable that the first person rappelling holds onto the rope at the belay station so that it does not swing away or get blown away by strong winds, or gets caught up on a tree root or a bush.

If at the first belay stand there is still a lot of rope remaining, the first person takes the end from which the rope will be pulled in later and pulls it as much as possible through the next rappel anchor. This increases the overview and gains time, which could be an important safety aspect with approaching bad weather or at the beginning of dusk. In spite of this, one should always remain as calm as possible. Rush and hurry can lead to conflicts between the partners and create considerable risks.

Despite the accuracy of topos these days, it can always happen that the listed lengths of pitches are not correct. If the actual route is shorter than indicated, this should normally not pose a problem. However, if one of the pitches is longer than half of the length of the rope, there is only one possibility: The less experienced climber is lowered back to the base station. This is easy to do if the problem had been recognized during the ascent. The experienced climber rappels down to a suitable intermediate protection point, sets up a new rappell anchor and then rappels farther down. If the problem has been discovered while the first climber is actually rappelling, then he has to construct a suitable intermediate belay stand during the rappell. Which protection points can be used in these cases is decribed in chapter 8, page 168 ff.

339

TIP: *If you find you have missed a belay point and you are already several meters below it, you should not attempt to climb unprotected back up to it. The best solution is to carry on until you reach a solid belay point and make the following climber aware of the correct rappel point. Only in extreme cases and on very simple terrain should you use a fixed rope with a Prusik sling to climb up (Photo 339).*

CAUTION: *Never rappel into completely unknown terrain. If you get stuck, it usually means calling for help—assuming you have cell phone reception. Otherwise, you have to try to attract attention by shouting or using other types of signals (see Page 189). On longer routes it makes sense, therefore, to ensure that someone knows about your plans, and expects to be contacted at the end of the tour. If that contact is not established, a rescue mission will be inititated.*

10 Climbing and Movement Techniques

340

The basic movements and climbing techniques used in the gym are generally transferable to natural rock. However, since there are no colored handholds showing the route up, searching and finding suitable hand- and footholds up the route is of greater importance outdoors. Especially the recognition of good footholds and the ability to stand safely may initially be unfamiliar.

Because the outdoor beginner will lead climbing routes of lower difficulties, he will usually find the terrain to be sloping and heavily structured. You need good foot and stepping techniques to manage this—movements that are seldom used or practiced in the gym. The basic elements of the climbing moves, such as the change of the center of gravity of the body to take the next step, climbing with outstretched arms, the various grip and foothold techniques, mantel moves and stemming will be familiar to the gym climber. Only friction climbing will be new to them. Therefore, we will cover this to some greater detail.

The key to a good friction technique is the correct body position. On sloping terrain, i.e, terrain of less than 90°, the body's center of gravity in an upright position should ideally be vertically above the feet or the weighted foot (Photo 341). Beginners tend to lean against the rock face, giving them a feeling of security (Photo 342). In reality, however, the center of gravity is no longer over their feet and thus results in less pressure and friction on their footholds. In addition, the area of their footprint is now smaller than in the ideal position, and this further reduces the friction between the shoe and the rock face. An upright body position results not only in better contact to the rock, but also permits a much clearer view of their surroundings.

The feet should be placed about shoulder-width apart, since each step requires a shift in the center of gravity onto the supporting leg. Similarly, a sequence of small steps is preferable over a single big step. This is useful for moving the center of gravity, as well as the use of energy-saving push holds.

Because good holds or crevices are seldom found on friction slabs, push holds on indentations, bulges, and ledges can be used to reduce load on the feet and thus stabilize body position. The second hand can then use holds above head height with little of effort.

TIP: *The friction of the climbing shoes and the move of your body's center of gravity can be easily practiced when bouldering on a sloping rock face. This needs to done close to the ground, and with a favorably landing spot. Regular practice in friction climbing will result in more confidence in the adhesion afforded by your climbing shoes.*

In the shorter routes of sports-climbing areas, one rarely encounters chimneys, cracks, or dihedrals. These special techniques will be covered briefly just to be complete.

Wide chimneys and dihedrals are climbed by putting opposing pressure on the sidewalls, with the legs spread apart. This climbing position, with the legs splayed, affords a very solid and energy-saving stance. Even in the absence of hand- and footholds on the wall will climbing shoes remain firm on the rock, due to the opposing pressure exerted; often one can take the hands completely off the rocks and still feel safe. To climb higher, you support yourself with the hand on one side and bring the non-weighted foot up higher. The other hand pulls lightly, grasping a handhold above. If this technique is used alternately, the climbing style will be fluid and energy

343

saving. If there is no handhold in reach, one can support the body with both hands to one side (Photos 343-345).

A jamming technique to climb narrow chimneys (i.e., you push both feet against one side of the chimney and your back against the other side). This creates an opposing force, which wedges your body firmly. By placing the hands near your bottom you can take the strain off the body and lift it farther up. In this technique you often move your foot on the rear side with one hand placed on the wall you are looking at. Because there is little opportunity to practice in the gym, sports climbers mostly avoid climbing chimneys on natural rock.

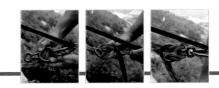

Similarly, climbing cracks is not typically in the gym climber's repertoire. Depending on the structure of the rock face, the hands are wedged into the crack, or they both pull on the side where one can hold onto. (Photo 346). If there are no good holds on either side, the hands are placed one in each side of the crack and pulled back against each other (Photo 347). The feet are placed either in the crack (Photo 348) or outside on climbable structures. At first, the gym climber will find these techniques rather exciting and extremely exhausting.

TIP: *If there are opportunities to practice climbing chimneys, cracks, or dihedrals, we recommended that, where possible, this is done from a top-rope position so that the appropriate techniques can be learned.*

11 Risks, Causes, Emergencies

An empirical study showed in 2005 that mountaineering and climbing belong to the sport disciplines that are associated with the lowest risk of injury and the best fitness gains. The risk of injury in soccer and volleyball was found to be 20 times higher (Randelzhofer & Hellberg, 2010). According to the German Alpine Club, the numbers of accidents in climbing and mountaineering has declined over the last few years although the number of people participating in these sports has increased. From a statistical point of view, this implies that the risk of injury while climbing has declined even more in recent years—in Germany at least.

Despite these positive statistics, climbing remains a sport with an inherent residual risk. It is up to each climber to minimize this personal risk, as "trained persons make less mistakes than those untrained" (Mersch, Trenkwalder, Schwierisch & Stopper, 2005). It is useful to know which kind of mistakes cause risky circumstances. A broad study on climbing sport, sponsored by the German Alpine Club, concerning number and frequency of mistakes in sports climbing shows the following: Most mistakes occur in belaying the lead climber. Nevertheless, only few lead climbers get injured because they control their own actions very well and make practically no mistakes in those instances. The critical phase for a climber is when he reaches an anchor point. Most accidents occur when repositioning, rappelling, and lowering (Klöstermeyer & Lade, 2011). This could be due to the declining concentration of the lead climber once he has accomplished a successful climb and believes to have passed the most dangerous part of the tour.

In addition to solid training within a climbing course the outdoor climber has to master the following topics when undertaking the first independent climbs,

- to judge his own limitations,
- to judge the challenges of a climbing route,
- to act correctly when falling and when holding falls, and,
- to consider extraneous circumstances properly.

Most risky situations can be prevented with sensible approaches and continually developing safety skills as well as tactically cognitive abilities,. Moreover, dangerous situations can often be mastered more easily if they have been considered beforehand. For example:

- How do I react to rockfalls?
- What do I do if I or my partner is injured during a climb?
- What do I do if the weather changes?
- How do I attract attention? How do I call for help?

Most accidents in well-protected climbing crags turn out to be not too serious and affect mainly the lower extremities. Most common are bruises and fractures, or sprains at the foot. With the help of his climbing partner, the injured person can be relatively easily brought to safety. For smaller injuries, one should always carry a First Aid kit in the rucksack.

If, despite all precautions, there is an emergency in climbing gardens, it is usually possible to lower the injured person down to the ground. In a multi-pitch route, this can also be done from belay station to belay station, provided the injuries are not too serious and the injured person is still conscious. Otherwise, the rope must be arrested and the rescue services must be notified (see Page 190). In many areas, there are locally organized rescue services and organizations. Depending where you are in the world when climbing, you must make sure you know the emergency number for that country. Even when networks are overloaded, these numbers will answer. They are also usually available, even on a prepaid cell phone when the money credit has run out. It is important to report the exact circumstances of the accident. When answering the five W-questions:

- Where exactly is the location of the accident
- What number of persons have been injured
- What has actually happened (Cause, type of injury)
- When did the accident happen
- Who is reporting the accident

one should particularly be able to exactly describe the location of the accident—either in the local language or in English.

349

If there is no cell phone reception, one should attempt to get help from other climbers or hikers. If is nobody around, one needs to rely on the "Alpine distress signal". This is done by calling, whistling, waving, or using a light signal (flashlight) six times within one minute. This is followed by a pause of one minute and then repeated again until you get a response. Anyone hearing the distress signal should reply with an acoustic or visual signal three times per minute followed by a one minute pause.

11.1 Locking the Belay Device

If the climber has injured himself so badly that he cannot be safely lowered, his partner must lock the belay and thus fix the injured climber before further actions can be initiated.

The locking of an HMS belay is done with a slip knot that is easily loosened when under strain. Because there are several ways of tying this and mistakes happen especially in stressful situations, the slip knot must always be secured with a carabiner or a securing loop (also called an overhand-bend loop). While keeping the brake hand on the brake rope, the slipknot is tied with the other, free hand. Photos 350-358 show how to lock an HMS belay when protecting a following climber. For a lead climber, the slip knot is fixed above the HMS in the same way.

CAUTION: *In the following situation, locking the HMS device is sometimes advantageous or even absolutely necessary: If the lead climber or follower is overchallenged and is resting frequently and for longer periods by hanging in the rope, and lowering down to the last belay station is difficult or impossible, as for example in a diagonal route.*

TIP: *Even when there is no emergency, outdoor beginners should practice tying the slip knot. Until you get the hang of the procedure, this can initially be done on the belay without load, until the procedure has been mastered. Tying the knot under load is distinctly more difficult and one should expect that the climber slipping a few centimeters lower until the slip knot blocks the HMS. To block a tuber device, you tie the slip knot round the shank of the carabiner that is connecting the tuber to the harness. This, too must definitely be secured by a securing loop (compare Photos 353-357) or by using a carabiner on the leg loop. A plate used to belay the following climber, is blocked with a slip knot in a similar way as for the HMS.*

12 Nature Conservation

"The quality a sport assumes depends on the motivation of the person practicing it. For instance, if a person climbs only for the sake of fame, prestige and his climbing will have no effect in generating peace of mind, tranquility and a deep sense of relaxation. However, if a climber exercises the sport with an appreciation for the beauty of the nature and the sense of responsibility and gentleness for the environment, his climbing can have a positive impact on his mental and physical well-being. Contact with nature gives people an opportunity to find peace from the restlessness of modern society."

(Dalai Lama, October 21, 1993; DAV, München 1996)

The relationship between nature conservation and rock climbing is marked by a discussion that forces the many positive aspects of the sport into the background. Critics tend to place climbing in the individual pastime category, which has to take second place behind the general interest of nature conservation. Climbers have always seen their rocky arena as a complete and whole, natural environment and have engaged themselves in preserving that environment. However, because of the great popularity of climbing and the resulting mass of climbing sportsmen practicing on the rocks, there are always many problems:

- Disturbing the animal world
- Damaging vegetation
- Thoughtless parking
- Polluting the rocky terrain

In the past, this was often the grounds for confrontation with conservationists and locals and led to exaggerated measures taken by regional political authorities, as several complete bans on climbing on rock terrain prove. Therefore, as an example in Germany, on the initiative of the German Alpine Club working together with conservation organizations and authorities, a climbing charter has been established that contains various routing measures and rules giving the framework for a way of climbing with conservation in mind. The German Alpine Club has created an information system covering 250 climbing areas in Germany. In the meantime, you can find websites for areas in France, Italy, Spain, and many other places in the world where you can find similar comprehensive information for that area.

360

Rock Climbing

Many climbing areas have various rules or tips about climbing certain routes in their area. The information on this can be found on several websites, for example in the USA have a look at the National Parks website under www.nps.gov, or for the UK, the British Mountain Council website under www.thebmc.co.uk/. These websites give information on climbing areas and the latest data on any forbidden areas or climbs. In Germany, the German Alpine Club has created rules for nature-friendly climbing, and we include them here as the rules are generally valid for anywhere in the world.

10 Rules for Nature Friendly Climbing

1. Abide by the up-to-date climbing rules.
Make sure you know the up-to-date rules for the area you are going to climb in—restrictions on climbs can be found on the websites or in good topo guides.

2. Adopt a conservationist viewpoint to get to your chosen climb.
If you use public transport or join together with others in one vehicle to get to your climbing area, you will ease the burden on the environment. Besides this you will save yourself the irksome search for a parking spot—parking is often scarce in climbing areas.

3. Only use official parking zones.
Thoughtless parking is not only a nuisance to locals or landowners, it is also a cause of damage to vegetation as well as perhaps offensive. Therefore please use the parking provided.

4. Do not stray from paths and tracks.
Woodland below the rocks often turns into steep screes. Because they are flat, these biotopes are particularly vulnerable to footmarks. Keep to the normal approach routes and take care of the indigenous plant life.

5. Preserve the vegetation.
Vegetation on the rock face is made up of a variety of small biotopes. Take care, therefore, when climbing over vegetation on rock and wall faces. Plant and animal life hiding in boulders in wooded areas is generally less spectacular, but nevertheless you should still take care when moving over such terrain. Avoid damaging shade-loving plant life, such as moss, lichen, and ferns as well as flowering plants.

6. Respect the forbidden areas.

Just below the summit of rocky climbs with sensitive vegetation, where you must take care, there are anchor and rappelling fixed points. Rocky areas, where climbing would damage such vegetation, are sometimes shut down by local conservationist authorities. Usually there will be some sort of sign indicating this. Don't violate these areas!

7. Hatching time = "No–go" times.

During hatching time for the rock indigenous bird life and when they are bringing up their offspring, temporary forbidden areas are announced. By respecting these restrictions, climbers can contribute to the preservation of rare breeds such as peregrine falcons and eagle owls. There will be signs marking these temporary "no–go" areas or you can find information on websites.

8. Do not leave your trash behind!

Thoughtlessly discarded trash not only disfigures the rocks, it is also an eyesore. Plant and animal life react sensitively to changes in their habitat. Therefore, your trash must not be left on the rocks. Any feces must be buried, and you should only use spots that indicate where you can light a fire.

9. Reap the benefits of what is offered!

Use local inns, B&Bs, or camping places for your overnight stops. This lets the locals benefit from the sport of climbing, and contact with the locals also helps to clear up any possible prejudices pertaining to climbers.

10. Refurbishments and Developments: Areas for Agreement.

In many climbing areas, working groups are actively composed of members from the climbing community and the conservationists. These groups consider what measures need to be taken to improve interests of both parties and thus ensure that, for the climbers, suitable routes are available that protect the environment and avoid conflict. Again, you will find details of this on websites or in the topo guides.

Appendices

1   Epilogue

We would like to conclude this book about rock climbing with some words that make it very clear why the adventure of this sport is really worthwhile. At the annual European International Mountain Summit meeting in Brixen (Northern Italy) in 2010, Dr. Siegbert Warwitz—a German psychologist and researcher on risk—gave a lecture with the title "The Right to Risk" (Recht auf Risiko) and his words succinctly bring the point home. Warwitz said:

Children who grow up freely learn quite naturally how to handle risk. Those that do so, with a relaxed, responsible relationship to risk, can handle it better than a politician or bureaucrat evaluating it from behind his office desk. This freedom is a person's right—even when mistakes occur. Deprivation of freedom incapacitates the human. Furthermore it is also prevents achievement and deprives one of the joy of experiencing self-determined growth and maturity. Freedom to venture out should be furthered, because one learns much from life and oneself in handling risk. Risk provides an impulse for top performance.

(Warwitz, 2011)

2   Grading System (Climbing)

Throughout the world, there is a variety of systems to grade the difficulty of climbing. The data you will find in the topos are an indication to the difficulties and are often laid down in relation to other routes. Because the degree of climbing skill difficulties cannot be measured on a unified basis, you will note that these vary from climbing area to climbing area and even sometimes within the same climbing route. Nevertheless, the data are very helpful and provide a good reference point for the beginner rock climber to find the most suitable climbing route for himself. The routes chosen for your first climbs in a new area should be at least one grade—better two—lower than your personal limitation.

In Central Europe there are various grading systems. In Germany, Austria, and Switzerland, the UIAA scale is used almost exclusively, and in very few instances the French grading system. In all the South European climbing areas (Spain, France, Italy, Greece and others) the French system is used. An exception is the Elbe Sandstone Mountains (German: Elbsandsteingebirge), a mountain range straddling the border between the state of Saxony in southeastern Germany and the North Bohemian region of the Czech Republic. Following an unusual tradition of climbing, the "Elbsandstein scale" has been developed there and includes its own climbing rules.

In the United Kingdom there are two different ratings: An adjectival grading and a technical grading. The adjectival grading (M, D, VD, etc.) indicates the difficulty of the climb. The technical grading (figure/alphabet) refers to the most difficult section of the route. For example, where a simple route includes a difficult section it would be shown with comparatively low adjectival grading combined with a high technical rating. In North America the grading system is known as the Yosemite Decimal System. In this system, the first number indicates the type of climb (for our purposes a figure "5") and the second number shows the difficulty.

The following table compares four various systems:

UK	UIAA	French	USA
M	3-	2	5.1
D	3	2+	5.2
VD 3a	3+	3	5.3
VD/HVD 3b	4-	3+	5.4
HVD/S 3c	4	4	5.5
MS 4a	4+/5-	4+	5.6
S/HS 4b	5-/5	5a	5.7
HS/VS 4b	5+/6-	5b	5.8
HVS 4c	6-/6	5c	5.9
HVS 5a	6/6+	6a	5.10a
E1 5a	7-	6a+	5.10b
E1 5b	7-/7	6b	5.10c
E2 5b	7/7+	6b+	5.10d
E2 5c	7+	6c	5.11a
E3 5c	8-	6c/6c+	5.11b
E3 6a	8	6c+	5.11c
E4 6a	8/8+	7a	5.11d
E4 6b	8+	7a+	5.12a
E5 6b	9-	7b	5.12b
E5/E6 6b	9-/9	7b+	5.12c
E6 6b	9/9+	7c	5.12d
E6 6c	9+	7c+	5.13a
E7 6c	10-	8a	5.13b
E7 7a	10-/10	8a+	5.13c
E8 7a	10/10+	8b	5.13d
E8 7b	10+	8b+	5.14a
E9 7b	11-	8c	5.14b
E10 7b	11	8c+	5.14c
E10 7c	11+	9a	5.14d
E11 7c	11+/12-	9a+	5.15a
E11 8a	12-/12	9b	5.15b
E11 8b	12	9b+	5.15c
E11 8c	12+	9c	5.15d

UK System legend: Moderate (M), Very Difficult (VD), Hard Very Difficult (HVD), Mild Severe (MS), Severe (S), Hard Severe (HS), Mild Very Severe (MVS), Very Severe (VS), Hard Very Severe (HVS) and Extremely Severe. The Extremely Severe grade is also broken down into 10 further sub grades from E1 to E11.

In order to compare the grading better, there are tables in practically all topos that cover the peculiarities of each of the climbing areas. Nowadays you rarely find the UIAA grading using the system of Roman numerals as it was common in the past. All the grading data is applicable for free climbing (i.e., where protection points are not used as gripping or stepping points). If this is done, however, then it is said that you are climbing the passage "technically". For this, there is also a grading system with values from A0-A4. "A" means "artificiel" (French) ("aid climbing" in english). A0 means that the climber uses a bolt or the attached quickdraw as a handhold (Photo 362) or foothold. With A1 and A2, one or two ladders are used to climb (Photo 363). A3 and A4 mean that there is no pitons or bolts in the climb, and that it is very difficult to place any protection.

If the climbing move is achievable either as free or technically, the difficulty grades will be shown for both. Example: 6- (5/A0).

3   Glossary

A

A0/A1-A4	*The A grading scale (A for "artificial" or "aid") for technical climbing—includes difficulty of fixing bolt mounting points, ladders, roping, and the danger associated with falling*
Aid climbing	*Technical climbing: using protection or anchors as holds*
Alpine	*Definition of a rocky area that is characterized by its height and mass and which represents a more serious climbing obstacle than e.g., a crag or climbing garden*
Alpine climbing	*Climbing in the Alps or Alpine regions*
Anchor	*Firm point in the rock to which one can use as a protection point at the end of a climbing route (e.g., bolt, chain etc.)*
Anchor carabiner	*Carabiner used with an anchor for rappelling or lowering*
Anchor point	*See Anchor*
Anchor protection	*Securing the partner's safety by using a safety device directly attached to an anchor point*
ATC guide	*A tubular belay device fitted with a plate function (i.e., an additional fitting for the climber's safety)*
ATC/Tuber/Tube	*ATC is a proprietary (Black Diamond) belay device designed to facilitate smooth feeding of rope—also called a "tube", "tuber", or "tubular" belay device*

B

Back-stepping	*Climbing technique where you climb with your side to the rock face*
Bailing out	*Withdrawing from a climb before reaching the end*
Barn-dooring	*Climbing technique where one climbs with one's side to the rock face*
Belay stand/station	*Point where a) the belayer stands at the base of the climb or b) the belay point when carrying out multi-pitch climbs*
Belay device	*See ATC /Tube; Figure Eight*
Belay loop	*A loop connecting your waist and leg loops on the climbing harness*

Bolt	*Artificial fixing point that is created by boring a hole in the rock and fixing the bolt in using a spreading dowel plug. Some plugs use a cement to create a sealing of the bolt*
Bouldering	*Bouldering is where you clamber over low rock outcrops in a horizontal manner, usually without the use of safety ropes*
Bowline knot	*Single and double rope knots. The single bowline is not safe while the double bowline is difficult to tie but is easier to undo after taking strain*
Brake (braking) power	*The friction (power) that the rappelling device is able to withstand without too much rope slipping through*
Brake hand	*Your brake hand is the most important hand for rappelling and is positioned just behind the rappelling device*
Brake rope	*The rope that is held by the braking hand behind the rappelling device*
Break strain	*Measured in kN (kiloNewton)—Carabiners come with a kN, or rating engraved into the spine*
Buddy check	*Checking your climbing partner for safety equipment*

C

CE	*Classification of safety applied to safety equipment, mainly used in Europe. The number following the "CE" mark shows which proof center is responsible for the classification. The international equivalent is the UIAA (Union Internationale des Associations d'Alpinisme) (English: International Mountaineering and Climbing Federation*
Cement bolt	*A bolt fixed by using cement or other adhesive*
CEN	*European Committee for Standardization (see also "CE")*
Central point	*A safety point at an intermediate halt where you or your partner can be secured to*
Chalk bag	*Small pouch for a climber's chalk*
Chalk ball	*Ball of chalk contained in a fine material, about the size of a tennis ball that allows a fine distribution of the chalk*
Chalk/Magnesia	*More accurate "Magnesium Carbonate"—used as a drying agent for the hands when climbing*
Chest harness	*Can only be used with a seat harness—prevents the body tipping backwards*
Chimney	*Crack in the rock that is more than 50-cm wide*

Cinch	*A semi-automatic rappelling device for advanced climbers*
Clean	*Clearing protection equipment from a route*
Climbing garden	*Smaller, well-constructed climbing area with safety fixing points*
Climbing guide see Topo	*Not to be confused with a mountain guide!*
Clip	*Clipping the rope to the carabiner*
Clip in	*Attaching the carabiner*
Clipping in	*Connecting the rope to a quickdraw express set*
Clove hitch	*Two loops made in the rope, the second passed behind the first. This knot is great for belays and making yourself safe*
COM	*Center of Mass—abbreviation rarely used*
Cord	*Thin rope with diameter 4-7 mm*
Counter pressure technique	*See Piaz technique*
Crack (Fissure)	*A fissure in the rock face that is less than 50-cm wide (c.f., Chimney)*

D

Dihedral/Dièdre	*An inside corner of rock, with more than a 90-degree angle between the faces*
Double rope	*Term describing all double-rope types (twin and half ropes) used in climbing*
Dr. Karl Prusik	*A professor of music and the inventor of the Prusik knot*
Drop shaped	*Particular form of knot in a granny or Figure Eight knot*
Dummy runner	*A fixed point above the intermediate protection point just above the foothold*
Dynamic safety	*Simple safety measures to prevent a hard fall*
Dyneema	*A mixture of polyamide and polyethylene to produce material for straps and slings made by a Dutch company DSM. Its destruction factor is considerably higher than the use of polyamide alone*

E

Eddy	*Semi-automatic belay device for advanced climbers*
EN	*European standard for safety equipment*
Eyelet	*Specially constructed eyelets on a bolt/piton*

F

Fall line	*Absolute vertical line under a point*
Figure Eight	*A belay device normally used for rappelling*
Figure Eight knot	*Roping-up knot*
Fisherman's knot/ One-sided overhand bend knot with a loop	*Knot used to tie onto a fixed rope*
Fisherman's knot/ One-sided overhand bend tightened	*Knot used to tie two ropes together—not easily freed*
Fixe carabiner	*Carabiner used as a runner at the end of a route (Made by FIXE)*
Free climbing	*Climbing technique using only aids required for safety protection and not those used to climb further*
Friction climbing	*Climbing technique using the friction between the rock face and the sole of the shoe to support the climber's weight, as opposed to using holds or cracks*
Full clove hitch	*See clove hitch*

G

Gear loop	*Loops or rings on the climbing harness to stow safety equipment on*
Girth hitch knot	*A knot used for fixing points—usually a clove hitch knot is used*
Grade of difficulty	*Grade of climbing difficulty*
Grigri	*A semi-automatic belay device for advanced climbers*
Grounder	*When the lead climber falls down to the ground*
Guiding hand	*The safety person's hand that feeds the rope (guide rope) in front of the safety device*
Guide rope	*The rope by the guide hand between the safety device and the climber*

H

Heel hook	*Using the back of the heel to apply pressure to a hold*
HMS	*Abbreviation for German word "Halbmastwurfsicherung", see Munter hitch*

Rock Climbing

I	
Intermediate protection	*All safety spots on a climb used by a lead climber (pitons, bolts, slings, tree roots or scrub)*
K	
kN	*KiloNewton; measure of force—equal to the amount of net force required to accelerate a mass of one kilogram at a rate of one meter per second squared*
L	
Lake Garda	*The largest of the Upper Italy lakes. Large area for rock climbing sport*
Lateral load	*Heavy strain of a carabiner in the transverse axis thus reducing its breaking point considerably*
Layback technique	*See Piaz technique Use of an artificial aid when climbing invented by Tita Piaz, a renowned alpinist; also known as Piaz technique*
Lead climbing	*Climbing a route where the rope does not run over a top rope anchor*
Lead rope	*The rope in the lead hand between the safety device and the climber*
Locking carabiner	*Twist or locking carabiner to protect the rope on a safe lowering*
Lower ring/gear loop	*The lower ring on the climbing harness to which the webbing rope for roping up is attached*
Lowering	*Lowering is a Rock Climbing Technique to descend or get down from a climb. A belayer at the bottom ensures that the climber is safely lowered—similar to rappelling*
M	
Marking	*Black marking or taped center marking of a climbing rope*
Mixed climbing route	*Climbing route on rock and ice*
Multi-pitch/Multiple rope-length route	*Climbing route using two or more rope-lengths*
Munter hitch	*A knot used to belay. Also called HMS (german for halbmastwurf, or "half clove hitch"*

N

No-hands rest	*Method for resting without using the hands*
Normal piton	*A piton hammered into a crack in the rock*
Normal weight	*A weight of 80 kg used in tests on climbing ropes*

P

Pear shaped (as in carabiner)	*Pear shaped: Specialized oversized offset-D's used in belaying*
Pendulum fall	*A small sideways fall by the climber*
Piaz technique	*Use of an artificial aid when climbing invented by Tita Piaz—a renowned alpinist*
Pigtail hook	*Special lower-off hook for top-roping*
Pitch/Rope length	*A pitch is the portion of a climb between two belay points or from start to top—hence rope length*
Piton	*A belay hook that is hammered into the rock rather than a bolt fixing; also called "pin"*
Plate/Sticht plate	*Tuber with the additional function of protecting the following climber—e.g., Sticht plate*
Polyamide	*Braided nylon material used to make ropes*
Prusik knot	*A knot used on a belay rope and with which one can be protected while rappelling or ascending*
Prusik knot for rappelling	*A Prusik knot used as a friction or braking hitch on a rope for rappelling*

Q

Quickdraw	*Two snap-gate carabiners connected together by a short sling*

R

Rappelling	*Free falling on a rope*
Rappelling route	*A prepared route on rock face for rappelling*
Redundancy	*Providing a back-up system by using a second one in case the first drops out*
Repositioning	*Sequence of handholds in order to e.g., prepare a suitable anchor position from which to rappel*
Residual risk	*The residual risk remaining where insufficient measures are taken in securing the whole risk*

Ring hook	*Special forms of climbing bolts with a large metal ring at one end*
Rock tunnel	*Two holes in the rock connected together*
Roof	*Horizontal overhang*
Rope abrasion/cuts	*Can be caused by friction borne when running over rough spots*
Rope sack/bag	*Appropriate covering to keep the rope from being dirtied*
Rope stretch	*The tensile strength of a rope constructed with properties to avoid and take the strain in heavy falls*
Roped party	*Team of climbers roped together*
Roping commands	*Short unmistakable rope commands for communication between climbers*
Roping up	*Attaching the safety rope to the climbing harness*
Route	*The climbing route indicated by preset fixing points and as shown in the topo guide*
Runner/Quick runner	*Material used to tie two carabiners together—as in a quickdraw*
Runout	*A lengthy distance between two points of protection*

S

Self-locking carabiner	*General term for carabiners—they have the same general shape as non-locking carabiners but have an additional sleeve securing the gate*
Self-securing sling	*Sling fixed to the harness for self securing on to a carabiner*
Series construction	*Connection between two fixed points to protect the belaying position*
Shock load/Impact	*The shock applied by the rope to a climber in a fall*
Single rope route	*A climbing route that is climbed without a break and normally is about 10 m and no more than 35 m high*
Slack rope	*Section of loose rope that is not taut in its run*
Slipper	*Climbing shoe without laces*
Smearing	*See Friction climbing*
Sports Climbing Centers	*Large climbing gardens often with multi-pitch routes*
Spotting	*Assistance usually with the hands given to lead climber. The spotter stands beneath the climber, ready to absorb the energy and avoid injury in a fall*

Spring-lock carabiner | *Carabiner without a locking device*
SUM belay device | *A belay device similar to a GriGri*

T

Tangle	*Twists and tangles in a climbing rope*
Tape sling	*Sewn webbing strip used for safety purposes*
Team/Roped party	*Team of climbers roped together*
Technical climbing	*Climbing involving a rope and some means of protection, as opposed to scrambling*
Tie-in	*Attaching the climbing rope to the harness*
Threading	*Threading the rope in preparation to rappel and/or lower down*
Toe hook	*A toe hook is securing the upper side of the toes on a hold. It helps pull the body inwards—towards the wall*
Top rope	*To belay from a fixed anchor point above the climb*
Topo	*A climbing guide including a sketch or diagram of a climbing route (originally 'Topo' as an abbreviation). Now found in all forms – photo/word or sketch form*
Traverse (Traverse passage)	*Part of a route that requires to climbed by zigzagging or climbing in curves*
Tuber/Tube	*See ATC*
Tunneling	*Slipping the brake-hand along the brake rope below the tuber*

U

UIAA	*UIAA (Union Internationale des Associations d'Alpinisme) (English: International Mountaineering and Climbing Federation)*
Unraveling	*Checking a rope with the hand along its length to unravel twists*
Upper ring/gear loop	*The upper ring on the climbing harness to which the webbing rope for roping up is attached*

V

Velcro fixing slipper	*Climbing shoe without laces fixed by using a Velcro sling*
Verdon Gorge	*The Verdon Gorge (in French: Gorges du Verdon or Grand canyon du Verdon), in south-eastern France (Alpes-de-Haute-Provence), is an impressive river canyon that is often considered to be one of Europe's most beautiful and best climbing regions*

Rock Climbing

Via ferrata/ Roped climbing area	*A climbing route pre-prepared with fixed ropes and ladders in rocky ground. Also called "Klettersteig"*

W

Waist harness	*Harness around the waist rather than a full harness*
Warm-up climb	*Climbing a relatively easy route to get the body and mind warmed up*
Webbing sling	*Connection made of webbing material between waist and leg straps on the harness*

Z

Zap-O-Mat	*Semi-automatic belay tool based on the tube style belay device*

4   Index

Rock Climbing

Appendices

5 Literature

Dalai Lama (1993). Quoted in DAV (1996). *Klettern – Ein Sport fürs ganze Leben*. München: Deutscher Alpenverein, 3.

DAV (2007). *10 Regeln zum naturverträglichen Klettern*. München: Deutscher Alpenverein.

Güllich, W., quoted in Hepp, T. (2004). *Leben in der Senkrechten*. Stuttgart/Nürnberg: Boulder Verlag, S. 8.

Hoffmann, M. & Pohl, W. (1996). *Alpinlehrplan* Band 2. München: BLV.

Köstermeyer, G. & Lade, P. (2011). Kletterunfälle im Frankenjura. *bergundsteigen, 11*, (3) 48-54.

Mailänder, N. (2010). Um ein Haar. *bergundsteigen 10*, (2) 30-31.

Mersch, J., Trenkwalder, P., Schwiersch, M. & Stopper, D. (2005). Hallenklettern. Ergebnisse einer empirischen Feldstudie. *bergundsteigen, 05*, (1) 58-63.

Randelzhofer, P. & Hellberg, F. (2010). Wie riskant ist Bergsport? *bergundsteigen 10*, (3) 42-48.

Schubert, P. (2011). *Alpine Seiltechnik*. München: Bergverlag Rother.

Semmel, C. (2009). *Übersicht Standplatzbau. DAV-Sicherheitsforschung*. München: Deutscher Alpenverein.

Warwitz, S. (2011). Wagnis muss sich lohnen. *bergundsteigen, 11*, (3) 40-46.

Würtl, W. (2009). Sichern 09. *bergundsteigen, 09*, (2) 76-81.

Zack, H. (2010). Mein Absturz in der Kletterhalle. *bergundsteigen, 10*, (2) 32-34.

6   Credits

Cover design:	Andreas Reuel
Cover photos:	Detlef Heise-Flecken, Lukas Loss, Dr. Peter Kamp
Internal photos:	Detlef Heise-Flecken, Gabi Flecken, Lukas Loss, Dr. Peter Kamp
Photo arrangement:	Lukas Loss
Copy Editing:	Elizabeth Evans
Layout:	Meyer & Meyer Sports
Typesetting:	www.satzstudio-hilger.de